"Africa's identity, influence, and independence depend on what we document now."

PUBLISHING AFRICA

Our Voice. Our Story. Our Future
A Wake-Up Call
Unless We Write It, We'll Be Erased by AI

GEOFFREY SEMAGANDA
Founder Publishing Africa

Copyright © 2025 Geoffrey Semaganda
All Rights Reserved

No part of this publication may be reproduced or distributed in any form or by any means without the prior permission of the author and/or publisher.

Kemp House
152 -160 City Road
London, EC1V 2NX
United Kingdom

ISBN: 978-1-917451-97-0
Published by Action Wealth Publishing
Printed and bound in the United Kingdom

Although the author and publisher have made every effort to ensure the accuracy and completeness of information contained in this book, we assume no responsibility for errors, inaccuracies, omissions, or any inconsistency herein. Any slights on people, places, or organisations are unintentional.

The material in this book is provided for educational purposes only. No responsibility for loss occasioned to any person or corporate body acting or refraining to act as a result of reading material in this book can be accepted by the author or publisher.

To my children Jonell, Tamiya, Zara, and Jed, thank you for giving me the space to seek answers and for the sacrifices you have made in the pursuit of this mission. Your patience, love, and unwavering belief in me have been my constant strength.

To my entire family and friends across the world, thank you for standing with me through every season and on every continent, for cheering me on when the journey felt long, and for reminding me why this work matters.

And to the dreamers, those who still believe the best is yet to come and continue to push for a better, kinder, and more just world, this book is for you. May your vision never fade and your courage never falter.

CONTENTS

ACKNOWLEDGEMENTS 12
INTRODUCTION 14
WHY I WROTE THIS BOOK AND WHY IT
  MUST BE WRITTEN 14
  Africans Must Be the Authors of Africa 19
CHAPTER ONE 22
THE AFRICAN SILENCE IN A NOISY WORLD .. 22
  A Continent That Speaks but Isn't Heard 23
  The Heavy Price of Silence 25
  Technology, AI, and the Coming Storm 26
  Storytelling Is Sovereignty 28
  We Are Not Starting from Zero 30
  The Movement Begins 31
CHAPTER TWO 33
WHY AFRICA IS MISSING FROM THE
  GLOBAL RECORD 33
  Colonialism and the Erasure of African Narratives 33
  The Myth of the Oral-Only Culture 35
  Economic and Structural Barriers to Publishing 35
  Language Loss and Linguistic Invisibility 36

Media Bias and Global Gatekeeping 37
Dependency on Foreign Publishing Infrastructure .37
Oral Tradition and the Risk of Loss 39
Educational Systems That Mirror Colonial
  Legacies 44
Brain Drain and the Flight of African Talent 46
Technological Exclusion 48
Cultural Gatekeeping and Internalised Inferiority ...50
Lack of Pan-African Collaboration 52
Economic Hardship and Limited Creative
  Investment 54
Breaking the Silence. 56
CHAPTER THREE 58
WHAT MUST BE PRESERVED 58
  1. Languages and Dialects 59
  2. Oral Traditions and Storytelling 60
  3. Traditional Knowledge and Innovation 61
  4. Spiritual and Religious Practices 64
  5. Cultural Expressions: Music, Dance, and Art 65
  6. Fashion and Textile Heritage 67
  7. Food and Culinary Traditions 69
  8. Architecture and Land Use 71
  9. Social Structures and Governance 74
  10. Historical Events and Resistance Movements ...76
  11. Philosophies, Values, and Ethics 78
  12. Diaspora Stories and Contributions 80
  The Cost of Not Preserving 82
  Towards a Preservation Agenda 82

Final Call: Publishing Africa, Preserving Ourselves 83
CHAPTER FOUR 86
IF WE DON'T PUBLISH, WE PERISH 86
   The Age of Artificial Intelligence: 87
   The Danger of a One-Sided Story 89
   If We Don't Document, We Can't Educate 91
   If We Don't Publish, We Lose Economic
      Opportunity 93
   If We Don't Publish, We Forget Ourselves 95
   The Geopolitics of Knowledge 96
   The Youth Will Inherit What We Publish 98
   If We Don't Publish, We Perish Politically 99
   Faith, Family, and the Soul of Africa 100
   The Time to Publish Is Now 101
   Africa Will Not Perish in Silence 102

CHAPTER FIVE 104
DOCUMENTATION IS WEALTH 104
   Stories Sell. Culture Pays 106
   Documentation Creates Jobs 109
   Publishing Builds Institutions that Outlive
      Individuals 111
   From Content to Commerce: Pathways to
      Monetisation 114
   Tourism, Culture, and National Branding 116
   Diaspora Dollars: Publishing Beyond Borders 119
   Women, Youth, and the Creative Economy 122
   The Cost of Delay 123

Conclusion: Wealth Is the Story You Own............ 124
CHAPTER SIX 125
WHO SHOULD PUBLISH AFRICA?...................... 125
   Individuals: The First Custodians of Memory. 126
   Families: Protecting Lineage and Legacy................ 127
   Communities: Archives of Collective Wisdom
      in Africa... 131
   Youth: The Digital Scribes of the New Africa. 133
   Women: Keepers of Culture, Custodians of
      Knowledge 135
   Faith Institutions: Recording the Moral Soul of
      Africa... 138
   Schools and Universities: Anchoring Truth in
      Education. 141
   Governments: Legislating and funding the
      National Memory... 143
   Publishers and Media Houses: Amplifying the
      African Voice.. 146
   Pan-African Bodies and Institutions 149
   The African Diaspora: Reconnecting Through
      the Written Word... 152
   Global Allies: Partners, Not Narrators 154
   Conclusion: Everyone Has a Role 156
CHAPTER SEVEN.. 158
PUBLISHING BEYOND BOOKS................................. 158
   Redefining Publishing in the African Context....... 159
   The Digital Renaissance: Africa's Time Is Now.... 160
   Visual Publishing: Art, Fashion, and Design 167

Theatre, Spoken Word, and Performance 169
Emerging Technologies: VR, AR, and Blockchain 173
Multilingual Publishing for Multicultural Impact... 176
Self-Publishing and Open Platforms 179
Building a Publishing Ecosystem, Not Just a Bookstore 183
Publishing as a Development Strategy 186
Conclusion: Publish the Message, Not Just the Manuscript 189

CHAPTER EIGHT 191

THE ACTION WEALTH PUBLISHING MODEL 191

From Pain to Purpose: The Origin of the Model .. 192
The Core Framework: Educate → Extract → Execute → Empower 196
A Track Record of Results 200
A Model for Publishing Africa at Scale 201
Why This Model Works for Africa 204
Publishing as an Economic and Social Engine 206
What's Next: Building the Infrastructure 208
Conclusion: Africa Can Publish Itself Systematically 209

CHAPTER NINE 211

LEARNING AND MASTERING THE AFRICAN NARRATIVE 211

Listening: Sound as a Tool for Memory 212
Watching: Visual Storytelling That Captures the Soul 214
Experiencing: Learning Through Interaction 215

Mastering: Teaching to Transform 217
Building Learning Ecosystems 219
Using Festivals, Schools, and Faith Centres 220
Monitoring and Celebrating Progress 222
Conclusion: Teach Africa to Learn from Itself 223

CHAPTER TEN 225
A CALL TO FUND AFRICA'S STORY 225
The Funding Gap: A Hidden Crisis 226
Why Fund Publishing? Seven Reasons
   That Matter 227
Who Must Fund the Story? Everyone. 230
How to Fund Strategically 232
The Publishing Africa Fund: A Vision for Scale ... 235
The Return on Investment (ROI) 236
What You Can Do Now 238
Conclusion: We Cannot Afford Silence 239

CHAPTER ELEVEN 241
THE FUTURE STARTS WITH OUR STORY 241
A Call Beyond Ourselves 241
The Reality Check: Africa at 2% 242
The Big Goal: From 2% to 20% 243
INDIVIDUALS: 246
SCHOOLS & UNIVERSITIES: 248
Knowledge that Builds Futures 248
GOVERNMENTS: 251
Documentation as National Security 251
CORPORATIONS & INDUSTRY: 254

Publishing as Legacy and CSR 254
FAITH INSTITUTIONS & NGOS: 257
Preserving Wisdom for Generations 257
THE DIASPORA: 260
Bridging Worlds Through Story 260
A Continental Vision: What a Published Africa
   Looks Like 262
The Real Stakes: Publish or Perish 264
The Final Call to Action: Your Role in
   Africa's Story 265
Conclusion: Write It Down or Watch It
   Disappear 266

CHAPTER TWELVE 268
BRIDGING THE DIVIDE: AFRICANS, AFRICAN-
AMERICANS, AND AFRO-CARIBBEANS 268
The African-American Journey in Context 270
The Afro-Caribbean Story 274
The Continental African Story 277
Myths and Misunderstandings 281
What We Gain by Learning Each Other's Stories . 283
Pathways to Reconnection 285
The Role of Documentation 287
A Vision of Unity 289
Conclusion: One Story, Many Journeys 291

CONCLUSION 294
WRITE IT DOWN OR BE WRITTEN OUT 294
Why This Mission Matters Now More Than Ever 295
Lessons from This Journey 295

A Pan-African Effort for a Pan-African Future 297
If We Don't Publish, We Perish Politically,
    Economically, Spiritually 299
A Final Word 299
ABOUT GEOFFREY SEMAGANDA 301

ACKNOWLEDGEMENTS

No great book is ever written in isolation. *Publishing Africa* is far more than words on a page; it is the culmination of a lifetime of lessons, the influence of countless mentors and changemakers, and the unfailing grace of God, who continues to guide and sustain me.

To my wife, Loy K. Semaganda, my best friend, my partner in purpose, the strongest woman I know, and the one who truly understands me. You have walked with me through every season and across every continent. We have fought together, dreamed together, and built together. Your courage in the face of challenges, your unwavering belief in our vision, and your ability to match my drive with your brilliance have made this mission possible. Every page of this book carries your imprint, your prayers, and your faith.

To the entire **Action Wealth Publishing** and **Publishing Africa** team, thank you for carrying the vision to help Africans and others worldwide publish their message, multiply their impact, and preserve their legacy. This work stands because of your relentless commitment to excellence and service.

To our clients, partners, students, and community members across more than 65 countries, thank you for trusting us with your stories and allowing us to witness the transformation that occurs when someone owns their voice.

To the next generation of African changemakers, storytellers, wealth builders, and future dreamers, this book is for you. Write it down. Record it. Film it. Share it. Teach it. The future is listening.

And finally, to every unsung African hero whose story was never written we will not let your voice disappear. We will remember. We will document. We will publish.

With deep gratitude,

Geoffrey Semaganda

INTRODUCTION

WHY I WROTE THIS BOOK AND WHY IT MUST BE WRITTEN

I was born in Uganda, but I was raised between two completely different worlds.

One was full of soul, where firewood crackled beneath cooking pots, stories flowed around smoky kitchens, and ancestral wisdom was passed down in hushed voices. It was a world of community rituals, cultural pride, and yes, war and conflict pain we carried but rarely documented. That world was alive but largely unwritten.

The other world, the one I entered when I moved to the UK, was cold but structured. It revolved around paperwork, processes, and policies. People there noticed everything. If a crime or accident occurred, someone could describe the person, what they wore, even what direction they ran. Because everything mattered and everything was recorded.

Libraries were everywhere, bookstores offered free reads, and even on the London underground, so reading a book wasn't just common, it was expected. I remember holding a book on the train just to fit in. Over time, I realised something profound: in that world, documentation was sacred. Records mattered. Data shaped perception. What was written was respected. What wasn't, was erased. Forgotten

As a sixteen-year-old, this was different from what I was used to in Uganda. I grew up during the chaos of war. Entire communities were shattered, families torn apart, but you won't read about that in textbooks. There's no museum exhibition, no national archive section to reflect on those years. It's as though it never happened. And yet, we lived through it. we remember it. But who will remember it after us?

That's why this book had to be written.

Too much of Africa's story is undocumented, and when you are undocumented, you are misunderstood. When you are misunderstood, you are undervalued. And when you are undervalued, the world moves on without you.

I've seen this happen my whole life. I didn't grow up thinking I was supposed to be wealthy. I thought wealth was something you prayed for. That if God really liked you, maybe you'd get lucky. But I also thought, does God love others more than us? Why are some people born into opportunities while others struggle to meet every basic need?

It wasn't until much later in life, after years of publishing books and helping others tell their stories, that I came to a deeper realisation: **documentation is wealth.**

We spend years educating our children about everything science, history, and careers, but we rarely teach them the foundations of wealth. Not just financial wealth, but the kind that begins with identity. True wealth starts with knowing who you are and how you see yourself. The less we understand ourselves and each other, the harder it becomes to succeed. Most conflict arises not from difference, but from disconnection. We've been divided, taught to see ourselves as separate, even inferior, so that others can take advantage of our confusion.

Power is documentation.

Those who document their lives, culture, thoughts, and systems own their narrative, shape their reality, and secure their place in history.

Those who don't disappear.

For a long time, even my own identity felt like a mystery. Growing up, I found that our education system never taught me to value this truly. Yes, we were taught elements of our culture, but never its significance.

We were told it was essential to study Shakespeare, but not our own griots. We learned about British royalty, but not our own kings. It wasn't until I began helping others document their stories that I had a powerful realisation: I couldn't guide others to tell their truth if I didn't know how to tell my own. That's when I began to understand my heritage wasn't just part of my past, it was a source of power for my future.

Now, every time I speak publicly, I proudly say, *"My name is Semaganda. From Uganda, in Buganda. A Muganda who speaks Luganda."*

However, it took me some time to reach that point. For years, I held back partly because of the tribal conflicts we've experienced in Uganda. I feared that embracing my identity so openly might make others uncomfortable. Nonetheless, over time, I learned something profound: people respect those who respect themselves.

In business, people do business with those they know and trust. No one can truly know you unless they hear your story. That's when it all clicked: knowing my story, owning it, and documenting it wasn't just personal pride. It was foundational to building trust, creating wealth, and making a real impact in the world.

I used to write books without really writing about myself. I would generalise. I would teach, but I would skip the rawness of my experience. However, over the years, I've learned something powerful: people connect with people. And people trust those they can see, feel, and understand.

Trust starts with truth. And truth must be told, not just felt.

I chose to go to the UK as a teenager, alone, not because it was closer or easier, but because it was familiar. I had read about it. I had studied its curriculum in school. I had watched its television programs and heard stories from people who had lived there. Britain was documented. Its systems, lifestyle, and culture were written, shown, and shared. Even at that young age, I felt

I could trust it because I had read about it in a paper. Now flip the script.

Why do so many people fear Africa? Why do even Africans sometimes fear each other? Why do people hesitate to visit, invest, or even take African voices seriously?

Because they don't truly know us, and the truth is, we as Africans often don't know each other as well as we should. That disconnect exists because we've done a poor job of documenting who we are, our stories, our strengths, our struggles, and our brilliance.

I once watched a story about Oprah Winfrey being denied service in a luxury store in Europe and again in New York. Oprah! The billionaire! Because they assumed she didn't belong. Why? Because of how she looked. Because she looked like us. And because Africa, the place many of us trace our lineage to, is still seen through a narrow, negative lens.

When the global elite gather to make decisions about the future, whether it's on climate, trade, migration, or technology, Africa is rarely at the table. In addition, when we are invited, it's often to agree with decisions that have already been made. Yet we represent nearly 20% of the world's population.

Something is deeply wrong with that picture. The problem is not our lack of contribution. It's our lack of documentation.

Africans Must Be the Authors of Africa

For far too long, we've waited for others to tell our stories, fund our projects, build our platforms, and preserve our legacy. But here's the truth: no one else will ever document Africa with the care, truth, and dignity that Africans can.

It is not the responsibility of outsiders to define us. Especially not those who benefit from our silence, or those who have no interest in seeing us empowered. We cannot keep asking the world to hand us tools to succeed when some of those very systems were designed to keep us dependent.

Africa's story is ours to tell. Its future is ours to shape. The responsibility to document, preserve, and publish African knowledge, history, culture, innovation, and identity belongs to us. We must stop waiting for permission or validation. We must stop blaming others for how we're represented. The world will always represent us in a way that serves its own interests unless we rise to represent ourselves.

Let us stop complaining about the narrative and rather become the narrators. We must build our own institutions, fund our own initiatives, train our own storytellers, and develop our own archives because no one can speak for us like we can.

We are not victims. We are visionaries. And it's time we act like it.

AI is now shaping the future of everything, including healthcare, education, justice, journalism, and even war and peace. AI learns from data. From stories. From language. From published content. If only 2% of that content comes from Africa, then AI is learning a world where Africa doesn't exist. That's not just sad. That's dangerous.

This book is my way of sounding the alarm and also providing a way forward.
You don't need to be an author to publish Africa.
You don't need a university degree or a publishing deal.
You need the courage to preserve, to share, to speak.
To write your truth. To record your people's story.
To pass on the wisdom that your ancestors whispered to you.

This book will show you why these matters matter, how to do it, and how we build an ecosystem across the continent to make publishing a part of our economic, cultural, and digital liberation. I've used this model to help over 750 authors and 2,000 content creators across 65 countries, as well as author and publish 8 business books and develop 20 different training programs. But this is different. This is about us. This is about Africa.

This is not just a book. It's a blueprint, a movement, a call to arms.

We must publish Africa because, if we don't, the world will continue to misunderstand us, ignore us, and exclude us. We've already been robbed of land, resources, and lives. Let us not be robbed of our story, too, because if we don't tell it, they will, and if they do, they will tell it wrong.

Let's change that. Let's publish Africa.

CHAPTER ONE

THE AFRICAN SILENCE IN A NOISY WORLD

Africa is home to more than 1.4 billion people, representing nearly 20% of the global population. According to United Nations projections, Africa's total population is expected to surpass 2 billion around the year 2038. Yet when we search for African stories, voices, and documentation in the global library of knowledge, what do we find?

According to UNESCO, Africa contributes less than 2% of the world's published content. This statistic is not just a gap in representation; it is a gaping hole in the global narrative. And with the world rapidly advancing into the age of artificial intelligence, data, and machine learning, that silence is becoming a dangerous void.

The future is being written by those who are documenting their past and present. AI is learning from what is available, and if African knowledge, history, innovations, languages, and culture are not present in that data, the future will ignore Africa. Worse, it will misrepresent her. We will be programmed out of existence not through violence or warfare, but through silence, the silence that comes from not writing, not publishing, not preserving, not archiving.

A Continent That Speaks but Isn't Heard

From the bustling streets of Lagos to the sacred shrines of Ethiopia, from the vibrant marketplaces of Kampala to the timeless wisdom of the San people in Southern Africa, Africa is rich in stories. Oral traditions, proverbs, music, and rituals echo with centuries of wisdom. But these echoes rarely make it into the archives of global knowledge.

Much of what Africa knows is stored in memory, not in media. It is passed down from grandmother to granddaughter, from elder to youth, from drums to dancers. This oral tradition is powerful and meaningful, but in the digital age, it is vulnerable. What is not written, recorded, or digitised becomes invisible to the algorithms shaping tomorrow.

Living Between Two Worlds

As someone born and raised in Uganda, where even the wars we lived through were never truly documented, and who has spent over three decades in the United Kingdom while traveling to more than sixty-five countries doing business, I've had the rare experience of living between two worlds.

One world raised me with stories told under the stars: stories of clans, warriors, spirits, and kings. These were more than entertainment; they were the oral libraries of our people. They shaped our identity, our values, and our worldview. But they were fragile, easily lost with time and death, because they lived only in memory.

The other world, the West revealed something very different. In the UK, I saw how power was preserved through paper. Everything was documented: history, politics, trade, culture, identity. Books filled libraries. Museums preserved centuries-old artifacts. Every small village had its story written and protected. Even opinions were archived in journals, films, speeches, and media.

In contrast, many of our African towns, kingdoms, inventions, and events remain unwritten. We carry them in our hearts, but the world cannot access our hearts. The world only respects and responds to what is written, recorded, and published.

That's when I realized something painful: the continent I love is not being left behind because we lack intelligence, creativity, or vision. We're being left behind because we haven't documented who we are.

Trust, Wealth, and Documentation

The consequences of that hit me the moment I arrived in the UK. I used to ask myself: How can countries like Britain or the United States, which borrow money month after month, year after year to cover deficits, still be considered wealthy? How can they maintain AAA credit ratings while living on debt?

Then it clicked: we trust them. We trust them more than we trust other nations. And why? Because they've documented themselves better. We know their systems. We learn their history. We study their institutions in our schools. Their stories are everywhere in books, films, news, and conversations. They are familiar to us.

That familiarity breeds trust. And trust is the foundation of wealth.

I didn't choose to go to China, India, or Russia. I chose Britain. Why? Because I knew more about Britain than I did about any of those countries. I knew the stories. I knew the system. The documentation made it feel like a safe and reliable place.

And I'm not alone. Many people across Africa make similar choices about where to go, where to invest, who to trust, based on what they've been taught, told, or exposed to.

That's when I understood: documentation is wealth.

The Heavy Price of Silence

When Africa does not write its own story, others write it for us. And more often than not, they get it wrong.

We've been portrayed to the world as a continent of poverty, disease, corruption, and conflict. These narratives are not always false, but they are incomplete. Yet they've become the dominant story not because they are the whole truth, but because they are the most documented.

That's the danger of silence. When you don't speak, others speak for you. When you don't write, others write you in or out however they please, then the world tends to believe the loudest, most persistent narrative, not necessarily the most accurate one.

This misrepresentation has consequences that go far deeper than embarrassment or image. It shapes foreign policy. It affects where aid goes, who gets funding, where investors look, and who gets overlooked. It impacts everything from tourism and trade to technology partnerships and global collaboration.

But perhaps the most dangerous impact is internal. When African children grow up without seeing themselves in books, in films, in textbooks, in history lessons, they begin to question their value. If their culture is never shown, if their history is ignored, if their voices are silenced, they begin to believe that they don't matter, that their story doesn't count.

Silence doesn't just steal our voice. It steals our confidence. It erodes our identity. And beyond the personal, there's a national and continental cost. The lack of documentation fuels division. When we don't record our shared history, values, or victories, we start to feel like strangers to one another. Tribes fight. Nations compete. Suspicion grows. Because where there is no understanding, conflict becomes the norm.

Africa is not inherently violent, divided, or chaotic. Much of what we experience is the result of people disconnected from one another, cut off from each other's stories. We've been scattered not just by colonisation or borders, but by a lack of cultural continuity. A lack of record. A lack of shared reference.

And that is the heavy price of silence. If we do not document our languages, they will die. If we do not preserve our customs, they will be erased. If we do not write down our stories, we will be written out of history.

Silence is not neutral; it's a tool of oppression. And our silence is costing us more than we know.

Now is the time to speak.

Now is the time to write.

Now is the time to publish Africa.

Technology, AI, and the Coming Storm

Artificial intelligence is not just coming. It's here. And it's rewriting how the world thinks, works, and decides. From healthcare to hiring, from education to elections, from agriculture to justice, AI is shaping decisions, policies, and outcomes across every sector.

At the heart of AI is data, and here lies the danger: these powerful systems are only as intelligent as the information they're trained on. They don't invent knowledge; they learn it from what's already available online.

And if 98% of that content is not African, then AI will not reflect us. It will not understand us. It won't recognise our languages, honour our values, process our context, or see our humanity. It will treat us like we do not exist.

Try asking a global chatbot to list African philosophers. You'll be lucky to hear more than one or two names. Search for African medicinal plants, traditional governance systems, or indigenous agricultural methods, and you'll find scattered mentions at best. Most of our wisdom isn't there, not because it doesn't exist, but because it hasn't been documented on a large scale.

This is not a technical error. It's the result of digital neglect. AI translation tools support hundreds of languages, but the majority of African tongues are nowhere to be found. Our accents are marked as "unrecognised." Our proverbs are lost in translation. Our innovations are buried beneath the weight of silence.

This absence will have lasting consequences. AI is already determining who receives loans, who is eligible for visas, which students are flagged for plagiarism, what content is promoted online, and how people are profiled in court. These systems are being built now, and once they're set, they will become harder and harder to reverse.

If Africa remains undocumented, we will be digitally invisible, and that invisibility will become exclusion. We will be excluded from economic models, language tools, research systems, academic references, innovation platforms, and global narratives. We won't just miss out on opportunities; we will be locked out of our own future.

The world will continue building the tools of tomorrow using only the voices of those who were loudest today. If we are silent now, tomorrow will not speak our name.

This is the storm we face.
Making publishing our only shelter.
Documentation our defence.
And content our currency.

We must not treat publishing as a luxury. It is a necessity. It is not about vanity; it is about survival, inclusion, and influence. Every story you write, every video you post, every article you publish, every language you preserve, every proverb you translate is a line of code that tells the future who Africa really is.

If we do not write ourselves into the database of human knowledge, then AI and the future it is building will write us out.

Storytelling Is Sovereignty

Storytelling is not just cultural. It is strategic. It is not just a way of preserving the past; it is a tool for shaping the future.

The nations that control the narrative often control the world. They shape what is considered truth, what is taught in schools, what is shown in the media, and what becomes policy. That's why Hollywood is more than just a film industry; it is an empire of soft power. It exports American ideals, values, and perspectives to every corner of the globe.

It's why British textbooks still echo colonial justifications because those who wrote the books got to frame the story. They didn't just record history; they edited it to suit their agenda. And generations of minds were shaped through that lens.

It's why global tech platforms set the standard for "normal" behaviour, "violations," or "community guidelines" because their systems are programmed with the cultural values of their creators. Even their algorithms have bias. And if we are not shaping those narratives, we are being shaped by them.

This is the power of storytelling. It is the power to define reality. It is the power to declare what is worthy, what is shameful, what is possible.

Suppose Africa wants to participate in the future not just as consumers, but as contributors, creators, and decision-makers. In that case, we must invest in the tools of narrative sovereignty, books that tell our stories, media that reflect our truth, curricula that teach our children who they are, archives that preserve our voices, platforms that empower our creators, and language technologies that protect and promote our dialects.

We must stop outsourcing our identity.
We must stop waiting for permission or recognition.
We must stop allowing others to narrate our existence.

Because when you don't control your story, you give someone else the power to define your value. The world doesn't just need to hear about Africa. It needs to hear from Africa on our terms, in our voice, and through our own platforms. Publishing is not just a profession. It is a form of self-governance. It is how we reclaim our name, reframe our narrative, and rewrite our future.

Africa must become the publisher of its own story. Not tomorrow. Now.

We Are Not Starting from Zero

Let's be clear: Africa is not a blank page. We are not empty. We are not late. We are not behind. We are a library that has not yet been catalogued. A museum that has yet to be curated. A symphony the world has never fully heard, not because it lacks beauty, but because it has never been properly recorded.

Our stories exist. Our knowledge exists. Our brilliance has always been here. But it has been scattered, isolated, hidden, and often undervalued even by us.

Across the continent, historians are delving into our past, authors are capturing our present, and technologists are building our future. Researchers are preserving indigenous wisdom, artists telling visual stories, elders who carry libraries in their memories, and young innovators creating platforms from Kigali to Accra to Nairobi.

However, many of them are underfunded, underrecognized, and under-supported. Their work is often invisible, not because it lacks merit, but because it lacks a megaphone. That must change. We are not starting from zero. We are starting from an abundance that needs to be organised, amplified, and sustained.

This book, *Publishing Africa*, is more than just a project. It is a manifesto for cultural sovereignty and a blueprint for reclaiming control of our narrative. It is a call to action for every African who refuses to let the future forget us.

It is for every mother who wants her child to see themselves in their textbooks. For every entrepreneur who wants to build on the legacy of African excellence.

For every educator who knows our minds cannot grow if we're only fed foreign stories. For every institution that believes in justice, truth, and equality, not just in principle, but in preservation.

Because if we do not write our stories, others will, and they will always define us by our weakest moments. They will zoom in on our scars and skip over our survival. They will spotlight our failures and silence our genius.

When we tell our truth fully, richly, proudly, and in our own voice, we don't just reclaim our narrative. We reclaim our power. We rewrite what it means to be African. We reframe how the world sees us. And more important, we help the next generation see themselves not through the eyes of pity or propaganda, but through the lens of pride, purpose, and possibility.

This is our moment to document Africa not as it has been described, but as it truly is and as it's destined to become.

The Movement Begins

What you're holding is not just a book. It's the beginning of a movement. A shift in mindset. A call to reclaim what has been ignored, erased, or suppressed for far too long.

In the chapters ahead, we will explore what must be documented, from our languages, histories, and customs to our innovations, leadership, and lessons. We will look at who must document it, not just scholars and writers, but families, faith leaders, educators, entrepreneurs, elders, youth, and the diaspora.

We will examine how to build the platforms, systems, tools, and institutions that make African publishing sustainable and scalable. And we will understand why publishing must evolve from a cultural project into a full-fledged economic, technological, and political revolution.

Publishing Africa is not only about paper and print, but also about pride in owning who we are without apology. It is about presence being visible, known, and respected in the global narrative. It is about power because the pen is still mightier than the sword, and the published voice still shapes policies, perceptions, and possibilities.

This movement doesn't require everyone to be an author. It begins with a pen, yes, a mic, a lens, a keyboard. These tools represent the courage to speak your truth, record your knowledge, and share it with others.

It begins when we decide that silence is no longer acceptable. That invisibility is no longer an option. Africa will no longer be left out of the archives that shape the future.

Let the silence end. Let the truth be told. Let Africa be heard.

And let you be part of the movement that made it happen.

CHAPTER TWO

WHY AFRICA IS MISSING FROM THE GLOBAL RECORD

To understand why publishing Africa is urgent, not optional, we must confront a painful truth: Africa's underrepresentation in global knowledge systems is not accidental. It is the outcome of centuries of structural, intentional, and psychological exclusion.

This chapter does not recount history for history's sake. It is a diagnosis, a clear-eyed examination of the root causes of Africa's absence in the world's archives, libraries, textbooks, databases, and digital platforms. Only by naming these forces can we begin to intentionally, strategically, and collectively reverse them.

This is not about pity; it is about power. Because if we do not publish ourselves, others will write over us.

Colonialism and the Erasure of African Narratives

Colonisation was not just a political takeover; it was an epistemic war. It declared African ways of knowing, remembering, and teaching as illegitimate. It dismantled entire systems of oral tradition, ancestral authority, and indigenous education.

From the mid-1800s through the twentieth century, colonial administrators and missionaries introduced European languages and values as the "civilised" norm. African languages were labelled as backward, spiritual systems were demonized, and local names were replaced with colonial identifiers.

Traditional historians, griots, elders, praise poets, and custodians of oral memory were ignored or silenced. In many places, ritual sites, royal archives, and sacred symbols were destroyed or looted, never to be returned. Some were taken to museums in Europe, where they remain as stolen relics with minimal context.

Colonial education systems taught African children to memorize the exploits of Vasco da Gama and Queen Victoria while forgetting their own kings, queens, prophets, and inventors. History was reduced to a pre-colonial "dark age" followed by a "civilising" mission, deliberately reinforcing the idea that Africa began with foreign intervention.

This wasn't educational malpractice; it was narrative engineering, a systematic erasure of African memory to justify foreign domination, and the consequences still echo today: many African schoolchildren still graduate knowing more about Shakespeare than about Chinua Achebe, more about Napoleon than Shaka Zulu, and more about European revolutions than African liberation movements.

The Myth of the Oral-Only Culture

Africa is often described as having "no writing" or being "purely oral." But this is a distortion. African civilisations had systems of documentation long before colonialism, from Ethiopian Ge'ez manuscripts to the Ajami script in West Africa, Nsibidi symbols in Nigeria, and the hieroglyphic and Coptic records of North Africa.

The libraries of Timbuktu held tens of thousands of manuscripts in astronomy, medicine, philosophy, and jurisprudence, many of which remain hidden or unpreserved due to neglect, theft, or lack of funding. The Kingdom of Buganda kept court records, legal decisions, and genealogies. The Swahili Coast had written trade agreements and literature in Kiswahili and Arabic.

Colonisers did not value or recognise these forms. They privileged Roman script and European formats, branding African systems as non-literate. And because many African societies used communal and oral models of memory embedded in rituals, ceremonies, and speech, colonial scholars dismissed these as inferior, "unrecorded," or "primitive."

In truth, Africa had memory keepers. We didn't always call them "authors."

Economic and Structural Barriers to Publishing

Even after independence, African voices remained largely excluded from global publishing ecosystems. Publishing requires infrastructure: printing presses, paper, publishing houses, editors, distribution networks, copyright frameworks, bookstores, literacy programs, funding, and digital access. In many African nations, these elements remain underdeveloped or heavily dependent on foreign aid and influence.

As a result, the majority of African thought leaders, creatives, and storytellers face massive obstacles. Books printed abroad are too expensive to be sold locally. Local publishers are underfunded and struggle to expand their operations. Western publishers dominate global markets and often dictate which African stories get told, and how. African authors are frequently asked to write from a lens of poverty, trauma, or exoticism to appeal to Western tastes.

The result? A global publishing system where less than 2% of the world's published content originates from Africa, despite the continent holding nearly 20% of the world's population.

This is not a lack of talent. It is a lack of access.

Language Loss and Linguistic Invisibility

Africa is home to over 2,000 languages, a rich tapestry of expression, worldview, and thought. But many of these languages are undocumented, unstandardized, and unwritten. Each time a language disappears, an entire way of understanding the world dies with it.

Colonial and postcolonial policies often prioritised European languages (English, French, Portuguese) for "development" and governance. Indigenous languages were sidelined in education, administration, and media.

This linguistic erasure means that most African stories are not being recorded in the language of the people who lived them. As a result, oral traditions are lost in translation, cultural meaning is diluted, and children grow up thinking that only English or French holds intellectual value.

In the digital age, this has devastating consequences: AI, algorithms, and search engines rely on written language. If your language is not digitised, indexed, or widely published, your worldview is invisible to the systems shaping the future.

Media Bias and Global Gatekeeping

Even today, global media and publishing gatekeepers shape how Africa is perceived and ignored. The editorial boards of major global journals, newspapers, and book awards are rarely comprised of African individuals. Publishing deals, speaking opportunities, and book translations are still centred in New York, London, and Paris.

African stories are often filtered through a deficit lens: war, corruption, and poverty. Stories of innovation, philosophy, faith, healing, and everyday brilliance are deemed "unmarketable." This skewed representation distorts reality not just for outsiders, but for Africans themselves.

Dependency on Foreign Publishing Infrastructure

Africa's story has long been told through borrowed microphones. For decades, what the world reads, sees, and believes about Africa has been mediated by foreign publishing houses, academic institutions, NGOs, and media conglomerates. These platforms often operate with their own priorities, financial, editorial, and ideological, and though some are well-meaning, the result is a fragmented and filtered narrative of Africa.

From academic textbooks to popular memoirs, Africans have too often been the subject, not the author. Anthropologists, missionaries, journalists, and foreign aid workers have written extensively about Africa's poverty, wildlife, corruption, and chaos, while African voices remain largely under published or marginalised.

This is not a visibility problem. It is an ownership problem.

When African ideas, innovations, histories, and cultures are published abroad, copyrights are owned by foreign companies. Revenue from sales rarely returns to the continent. African knowledge is often decontextualised or simplified to fit external narratives. Academic citations and cultural influence are credited to non-African institutions.

Meanwhile, local publishers struggle to survive. The cost of paper and printing is high. Funding is scarce. Bookstores are limited. Distribution networks are weak. Many governments have not prioritised national publishing ecosystems, meaning local writers are often forced to seek validation or opportunities abroad to be "seen."

Even those who publish independently often face a second layer of exclusion. Foreign-dominated search engines, social media algorithms, and online bookstores prioritise popular Western content, overshadowing African stories beneath a digital avalanche of global noise.

In this dependency, Africa becomes a guest in its narrative. Our children read books imported from Europe. Our scholars publish in foreign journals to gain credibility. Our voices must be translated and repackaged to be heard on the global stage.

This is not sustainable. We must build a publishing infrastructure that serves African needs, honours African perspectives, and rewards African creators. That means investing in local publishing houses, editors, and literary agents; creating affordable printing and distribution systems within the continent; building online platforms that prioritise African voices and languages; protecting African intellectual property and ensuring creators benefit from their work; and training a new generation of culturally grounded publishers, designers, and curators.

Africa cannot rely on foreign platforms to tell its story and then complain about misrepresentation. Until we own the means of production, we do not own the narrative.

This chapter in Publishing Africa is a call to break the dependency not with hostility, but with strategy. It is time to shift from consumption to creation, from reaction to authorship, from borrowing to building.

Oral Tradition and the Risk of Loss

Africa is a continent of memory. For centuries, our knowledge has been spoken, not written, passed down through proverbs, songs, folktales, rituals, and communal storytelling. From griots in West Africa to praise poets in Southern Africa, our elders were our living repositories of knowledge.

Oral tradition is not a weakness. It is a treasure. It is dynamic, flexible, and deeply rooted in the community. It allows knowledge to adapt to context, to be performed, lived, and felt. Through it, we have preserved histories of kings and migrations, tales of creation and morality, genealogies, philosophies, and survival tactics, all without books.

But in today's digital, data-driven world, what is not recorded is often deemed non-existent. Search engines, AI models, educational systems, and global databases do not understand oral wisdom unless it is captured in a form they can read, sort, and replicate.

As elders pass away without recording their stories, entire lineages of knowledge disappear. A folktale not retold becomes a silence. An undocumented ritual becomes a rumour. A proverb forgotten becomes a gap in our cultural DNA.

And this loss is accelerating. Modern life separates youth from elders, reducing opportunities for oral transmission. Urbanisation breaks traditional settings where stories were shared around fires, during harvests, or at community gatherings. Formal education privileges written texts, foreign languages, and "universal knowledge." Globalisation saturates our attention with imported entertainment, displacing indigenous storytelling rhythms.

Oral tradition is alive but fragile. It cannot survive on nostalgia alone. It must be intentionally preserved, recorded, and honoured in formats that bridge the past and the future.

This does not mean abandoning oral culture, but amplifying it through technology and publication. We need audio documentaries and podcasts in local languages, transcriptions and translations of elder interviews, illustrated children's books based on indigenous folktales, video recordings of songs, dances, and rituals, community storytelling festivals documented and archived, and AI models trained on African oral content, not just Western texts.

We must treat our elders as national archives and storytellers as scholars. Every village holds a library waiting to be recorded. If we do not act, the risk is not just cultural loss. It is historical extinction. And once a language dies or a story vanishes, it cannot be Google-searched. It is gone forever. Preserving oral tradition is not about resisting the future; it's about making sure we're part of it.

The Urgency of Archiving: Preserving Africa's Memory and National Heritage

Across the continent, millions of pages of African history sit in boxes, storerooms, and forgotten libraries. University theses written during the 1960s independence period are rotting away. Old newspapers that recorded the birth of nations lie in piles, fading to dust. Church baptismal records, land deeds, family letters, and government reports once the heartbeat of our societies now sleep in damp basements, eaten by termites, neglected by time. These are not just old papers, they are the memory of Africa's soul the proof of what we have done, believed, and achieved. When they are lost, a piece of who we are disappears forever. And when we fail to preserve them, we hand over our history, and our voice, to others.

A nation without memory is a nation without direction. And yet, across much of Africa, documentation and archiving are treated as optional luxuries rather than foundational pillars of nation-building and development. Many African countries lack comprehensive, well-funded national archives. Where archives do exist, they are often under-resourced, understaffed, and technologically outdated. Some are housed in dilapidated buildings, with critical historical documents treaties, constitutions, speeches, and manuscripts stored in crumbling boxes, exposed to humidity, insects, and political neglect.

Libraries and museums face similar crises. Books go out of print with no digital backups. Indigenous maps, land records, and cultural artefacts are lost, stolen, or hoarded in private collections. Important photographs, letters, and audiovisual materials from independence movements and liberation struggles are inaccessible to the public or worse, missing altogether. In some cases, entire colonial archives were shipped back to Europe, leaving post-independence governments with no original records of land agreements, tax laws, or diplomatic history. Even now, efforts to repatriate African archival material are slow, politically complicated, and poorly funded.

But this is more than a cultural tragedy it is a developmental crisis. Without national memory banks, governments repeat past policy mistakes. Land disputes persist because ancestral boundaries are undocumented. Youth are disconnected from the nation's founding vision. Researchers lack reliable data to inform development plans. AI systems and global databases continue to operate with gaps in African representation.

When history is not archived, corruption thrives, disinformation spreads, and nationhood becomes shallow. A society without access to its own records cannot fully understand its achievements, mourn its losses, or protect its sovereignty.

And the crisis is not only physical. Digital preservation is almost entirely missing. Few African countries have robust digitisation projects, and those that do are often funded externally, with little control over where the data lives or how it's used. In a world rapidly moving into cloud-based intelligence and blockchain certification, our histories are stuck in file cabinets if they exist at all.

To truly publish Africa, we must reimagine archiving as infrastructure, not just heritage. That means funding and modernising national archives, creating decentralised regional repositories for culture, history, and knowledge, training professional archivists, curators, and digital librarians, digitising fragile and endangered records with urgency, and establishing public access to archives not just for scholars but for communities and students.

This is not merely about saving the past; it is about empowering the future. A documented people is a dignified people. An informed nation is an archived nation. We must not allow our stories to disappear between generations for if we do not preserve them, someone else will write them, and in doing so, rewrite us.

Educational Systems That Mirror Colonial Legacies

Education should be a tool for liberation, but across much of Africa, it remains a subtle instrument of alienation. Our current school systems, in terms of structure, content, and philosophy, still carry the blueprint of colonial design. They were not originally built to empower African minds; they were designed to control them.

Decades after independence, many African countries still operate curricula that prioritise European histories, literature, languages, and logic systems, while neglecting indigenous knowledge, languages, philosophies, and innovations. In many schools, children can recite Shakespeare but know nothing of Chinua Achebe. They learn about the Industrial Revolution, but not the golden age of Timbuktu or the ironworking traditions of the Nok.

This colonial carryover is not just academic; it is psychological.

When a child is taught that knowledge is limited to English or French…

When they are evaluated by how well they can reproduce foreign concepts rather than think critically about their own context…

When they are discouraged from speaking their mother tongue at school or expressing traditional beliefs…

Then education becomes a form of disconnection, not enlightenment.

This creates a cycle of silence and dependency. African students graduate with a limited understanding of their history and intellectual heritage. They rely on Western sources for authority and validation. Local knowledge systems often go undocumented because they're not considered "academic." Generations grow up feeling inferior to imported ways of thinking.

And the result? An Africa that remains intellectually dependent even as it rises economically. Even science and innovation are not spared. Indigenous medicine, sustainable agriculture, architecture, astronomy, and conflict resolution systems, many of which are deeply rooted in African practice, are rarely integrated into mainstream education. We teach imported models while ignoring the knowledge that has kept African societies resilient for centuries.

Meanwhile, languages of instruction remain a major barrier. Most African children are educated in a language they do not speak at home. This creates early disadvantage, kills confidence, and undermines comprehension. Language becomes a gatekeeper, not a bridge.

To change this, we must decolonise education, not by rejecting global knowledge, but by placing African thought at the centre of the learning process. That means reforming national curricula to include African history, literature, and philosophy as core, not elective, subjects. It means training teachers to value and integrate indigenous knowledge. It means encouraging research in local contexts, in local languages. It means publishing textbooks, storybooks, and academic material authored by Africans for African learners.

Multilingual education, where mother tongues are respected rather than punished, must be promoted. We must redefine what it means to be "educated" in African societies.

Education is the root of all national development. But if the roots are foreign, the fruit will never truly be ours.

Brain Drain and the Flight of African Talent

Africa is rich in brilliance, but much of that brilliance is forced to shine elsewhere.

The phenomenon of brain drain through the migration of Africa's best minds to countries with better funding, infrastructure, and opportunity has long been a silent leak in the continent's intellectual future. While the diaspora contributes in many ways, the absence of these thought leaders on the ground weakens local institutions, cultural transmission, and documentation efforts.

Thousands of African scholars, researchers, writers, scientists, and artists now live and work in foreign universities, studios, and think tanks. Many of them publish groundbreaking research, produce world-class art, and influence global discourse. However, their work is often consumed abroad, framed through foreign priorities, and largely disconnected from African audiences and challenges.

This separation has serious consequences. Young Africans lack visible, local role models who embody intellectual and creative excellence within their own context. African institutions lose mentorship, innovation, and leadership needed to build sustainable academic and publishing ecosystems.

Knowledge created by Africans is often inaccessible to Africans locked behind expensive academic paywalls or published in Western languages and platforms. Cultural and historical documentation becomes externally mediated, filtered through the lens of the host country or global market forces.

The result is a paradox: Africa produces the minds but rarely retains the legacy. The continent remains a source of raw intellectual material, exported like a natural resource, only to be processed, refined, and validated elsewhere.

And while digital connectivity has made global collaboration easier, it is no substitute for rooted, local presence. The continent needs its historians to walk its land, its linguists to hear its dialects firsthand, its philosophers to wrestle with African realities in African spaces, its publishers to invest not just in exporting stories, but in grounding them.

To reverse this trend, we must do more than call our talent home; we must create a continent worth staying for. That means investing in local publishing houses, academic journals, and creative platforms; offering funding, grants, and recognition for work that documents African knowledge and culture; building infrastructure that supports long-term research, writing, and public engagement; reforming visa, tax, and procurement policies that make it hard for Africans abroad to contribute meaningfully back home; and creating hybrid residency programs and diasporic fellowships that bridge global exposure with local impact.

Africa cannot afford to keep losing its scribes, scholars, and sages. The future will not remember those who left; it will remember those who stayed and documented.

Technological Exclusion

In the twenty-first century, technology is the new printing press, but many African communities remain locked out of the tools that define the digital age. While the world races toward artificial intelligence, blockchain, and immersive publishing platforms, vast sections of the African continent are still struggling with stable electricity, basic internet access, and digital literacy.

This digital divide is more than an inconvenience, it is a barrier to authorship, visibility, and participation. Without computers, smartphones, affordable data, or cloud storage, millions of Africans are cut off from the platforms that now determine whose stories are told, whose voices are amplified, and whose knowledge is preserved.

In this era of algorithmic influence, if your content isn't online, it doesn't exist. If your language isn't indexed, your culture is invisible. If your data isn't digitised, your history won't be part of AI training sets or future global knowledge systems.

This is especially dangerous because modern publishing is no longer limited to printed books. Today, publishing includes blogs, podcasts, e-books, social media, academic repositories, digital storytelling platforms, and multimedia content, all of which require digital access and technical skills. In rural areas and underserved urban communities, these tools are scarce. Libraries lack computers or internet connectivity. Schools don't teach digital publishing or coding. Cultural institutions have not digitised archives or oral records. Traditional storytellers and artists lack the support to translate their work into digital formats.

Even among educated youth, the ability to produce content often depends on foreign-owned platforms that dictate format, visibility, and monetisation. Meanwhile, the algorithms that shape global search engines and artificial intelligence are being trained on what is already online. If African content isn't present, the future won't reflect us. AI will mirror our absence, misrepresenting or ignoring African perspectives entirely.

This isn't about access to technology. It's about access to the future.

To bridge this gap, we must invest in rural broadband expansion, community Wi-Fi, and solar-powered tech hubs. We must train youth and elders alike in digital storytelling, archiving, and publishing tools. We must develop African-owned digital platforms to house and showcase indigenous content. We must digitize endangered archives, oral traditions, and cultural heritage collections to preserve them for future generations.

We must promote digital literacy as a core part of education and national development. We must partner with universities, tech companies, and diaspora talent to support the development and dissemination of open-source African content.

Technological exclusion equals narrative exclusion. If we are not online, we are not in the room where the future is being built. Africa must not just consume technology; we must publish through it, innovate with it, and preserve ourselves within it.

Cultural Gatekeeping and Internalised Inferiority

One of the most damaging legacies of colonisation is not visible in maps or monuments, it is psychological. After centuries of being told that our languages, beliefs, aesthetics, and ideas were inferior, many Africans have internalised the lie.

Today, we often value what is imported more than what is indigenous, and this mindset quietly polices what gets published, praised, or preserved. This is cultural gatekeeping, a form of self-censorship that stems from internalised inferiority. We silence ourselves before anyone else can.

A writer may avoid using their mother tongue, thinking it lacks sophistication. A filmmaker may downplay traditional beliefs, fearing they seem "primitive." A researcher may cite European theorists while ignoring African elders and thinkers. A young poet may choose New York slam style over local spoken-word forms not because it's better, but because it's more "recognisable."

This is the colonial scar we rarely discuss: the belief that our knowledge must be filtered, diluted, or externally validated to be taken seriously. As a result, African stories are often rewritten for foreign approval. Local wisdom is undervalued unless endorsed by Western institutions. Traditional practices are performed in private but not published in public. Creative expression is shaped by what is "marketable" to outsiders, not what is true to self.

This mindset affects more than artists. It shapes public policy, education, media, religion, and development. Foreign consultants are trusted more than local experts. Imported frameworks are adopted before exploring indigenous solutions. And our children grow up thinking that success sounds foreign and looks like something for someone else.

The danger here is twofold: we begin to erase ourselves from our own narrative, and we block the next generation from believing their roots are worthy of being written. To change this, we must break the psychological gate and reclaim the authority to tell our stories not in imitation of the West, but in the full confidence of who we are.

That means affirming African stories, languages, and aesthetics as intellectually and artistically valid. It means encouraging writers, artists, and scholars to tell stories grounded in their communities. It means publishing local content for local audiences, not just for export. It means celebrating traditional knowledge systems as sources of innovation, not superstition. It means replacing the colonial gaze with an ancestral mirror, seeing ourselves through our own eyes.

As long as we doubt our own voices, we will keep looking for permission to speak. But no one owns our truth but us. Publishing Africa starts with believing in Africa.

Lack of Pan-African Collaboration

Africa is vast, diverse, and richly complex. Still, when it comes to cultural preservation and publishing, it too often functions as a collection of isolated islands instead of a connected continent. Despite our shared histories, linguistic overlaps, spiritual parallels, and mutual struggles, African nations rarely collaborate at scale to document and promote their cultural assets.

This fragmentation has serious consequences. Stories are lost across borders; what one nation forgets, another might remember, but the link is never made. Efforts are duplicated, as multiple countries launch small, underfunded archiving or translation projects with no knowledge of each other's work. Voices are scattered.

Instead of presenting a unified African presence in global forums, publishing platforms, or academic discourse, we appear as fragmented and underrepresented communities. Resources are wasted, as each nation works in silos, limited by local capacity.

Africa is not one country, but it can be one force. A [Pan-African publishing movement]() is not just a beautiful idea; it is a strategic necessity. The challenges we face, such as technological exclusion, language loss, lack of publishing infrastructure, and brain drain, are shared challenges. So too must be the solutions.

Let's translate African languages across borders: Kiswahili into Wolof, Zulu into Hausa, Luganda into Yoruba, and Amharic into Arabic, so no voice is confined by geography.

Let's unite publishers, universities, and archivists from Lagos to Nairobi to Dakar to create continental anthologies, oral history archives, and reformed curricula.

Let's link diaspora scholars and creatives from Brazil, the U.S., and the Caribbean directly to continental projects through a shared publishing platform.

Let's build a continental database of African-authored content, accessible to anyone, from anywhere, in multiple languages.

Let's secure African Union support for regional publishing hubs and digitisation labs across East, West, Central, Southern, and North Africa.

This is not a dream. It is a blueprint waiting to be brought to life. To get there, we must move beyond nationalism and a sense of pride of place. The preservation of Africa's story cannot be left to one tribe, one nation, or one language. We must think like ancestors whose vision extended across generations and geographies.

A Pan-African publishing strategy must create cross-border coalitions of writers, translators, editors, and historians; standardize digital tools, formats, and platforms to share cultural content continent-wide; host Pan-African festivals, fellowships, and residencies focused on heritage preservation; establish African-owned repositories and copyright frameworks that protect and monetize our collective output; encourage governments to fund regional, rather than solely national, cultural initiatives; and integrate diaspora voices into Africa's publishing future not as guests, but as family.

Africa's strength has always been in its diversity, but its power will lie in its unity of purpose. Fragmentation weakens us. Collaboration will write us back into history and into the future.

Economic Hardship and Limited Creative Investment

In many African nations, survival often takes precedence over storytelling. With pressing concerns such as poverty, unemployment, healthcare, conflict, and infrastructure challenges dominating national agendas, documentation and cultural investment are frequently dismissed as secondary or, worse, indulgent.

Ministries of culture, arts, and heritage are chronically underfunded, if not entirely symbolic. National budgets prioritise immediate needs and rightly so, but in the process, long-term memory is sacrificed for short-term survival. Writers are left unpaid, museums fall into disrepair, libraries become obsolete, and cultural initiatives struggle for relevance and support.

This scarcity trickles down to communities. Aspiring authors have no access to affordable publishing.

Historians are forced to abandon research for more "practical" jobs. Oral historians, griots, and elders often die unrecorded because no one has the time or tools to archive their stories. Local languages are not taught or published because it costs more to print in multiple dialects. Artists and creatives are told to "get real jobs" instead of being funded as nation-builders.

Yet this approach is dangerously shortsighted. Documentation is not a luxury; it is a strategic investment. It strengthens education, as local books, languages, and histories help students see themselves in what they learn. It fuels tourism, as cultural heritage draws visitors, generates income, and fuels national pride. It reinforces identity because documented people are harder to erase or misrepresent. It sparks innovation, since indigenous knowledge systems often contain untapped solutions to modern problems. It guides development, as accurate records, maps, and memory inform better governance and planning.

When culture is underfunded, the cost is paid in silence, confusion, and disconnection. Without stories, we lose the glue that binds nations, the wisdom that guides policy, and the spark that drives creativity.

Governments must begin to view the creative sector as a pillar of national development, rather than a distraction from it.

Breaking the Silence.

Now that we understand the historical and systemic forces that have kept Africa from the global record, from colonial erasure to economic neglect, from technological exclusion to internalised inferiority, we must confront them, not with complaint, but with bold, coordinated solutions.

We must decolonise education and place African knowledge, languages, and thinkers at the heart of our learning. We must fund local publishers and authors and build our own ecosystems of creation and distribution. We must create national and regional archives and treat memory as infrastructure, not as a museum piece.

We must digitise oral histories and rare documents, capturing the stories of our elders before they are lost. We must train the youth in documentation tools and empower the next generation to publish their truth. We must build networks of storytellers, scholars, and archivists, because collaboration is our greatest multiplier.

Africa's absence in the global record is not inevitable, but it will become permanent if we continue to delay. We are the generation with the tools to write ourselves back into history. We are the first to hold smartphones, video cameras, blogs, and AI models in our hands, tools that can record, preserve, and amplify like never before.

The question is: Will we use them? Because culture doesn't just die when it is attacked. It dies when it is ignored. We are the custodians of our culture. If we don't publish it, we perish with it.

CHAPTER THREE

WHAT MUST BE PRESERVED

If Africa is to reclaim its rightful place in the global narrative, we must begin by identifying and documenting the very essence of who we are. Before we digitise, publish, and archive, we must first understand what is sacred, what is significant, and what must never be lost. Our heritage is not limited to statues, monuments, or textbooks. It is a living, breathing, dynamic system of values, practices, expressions, wisdom, and memory passed down through generations.

This section is a catalogue of African wealth, not in minerals or money, but in meaning. It outlines the key elements of our cultural and intellectual inheritance that must be preserved.

These are the foundations of our identity, our creativity, and our resilience. If we fail to document them, we risk disappearing not only from history books but from the algorithms and archives that are shaping the future.

1. Languages and Dialects

Africa is the most linguistically diverse continent on Earth, home to over 2,000 languages and thousands more dialects. Each language carries a unique worldview, its way of understanding life, community, death, nature, and the divine. Embedded within our languages are philosophies, wisdom, humour, customs, and spiritual perspectives that have shaped entire civilisations.

Yet many African languages are now endangered. Colonial education systems prioritised European languages, while globalisation and urban migration have led many young people to abandon their native languages. Without urgent action, dozens of African languages could disappear within a single generation.

To lose a language is to lose a lens, a way of seeing, interpreting, and experiencing the world.

We must preserve:

- ✧ Oral histories and storytelling traditions.
- ✧ Proverbs, idioms, and metaphors unique to each language.
- ✧ Folktales, riddles, lullabies, and traditional songs.
- ✧ Grammar rules and written dictionaries.
- ✧ Bilingual and multilingual learning resources for schools.
- ✧ Voice recordings and transcriptions from elders and native speakers.
- ✧ Digital archives of regional speech patterns and accents.

African governments, linguists, educators, and creatives must treat <u>language preservation as a matter of national security</u>. Our languages are not merely tools for communication; they are vessels of knowledge, carriers of identity, and keys to intergenerational wisdom.

Language documentation must move beyond academia and become a household mission. Children should be taught to speak their mother tongue with pride. Communities can host language days, record elders speaking in dialect, and upload local sayings to public repositories.

Language apps, eBooks, and YouTube channels must be developed in African languages. Because when we lose a language, we don't just lose words, we lose a way of being. This is only the first item in our cultural treasure chest. The next step is to document what else makes Africa whole, brilliant, and enduring.

2. Oral Traditions and Storytelling

Long before the printing press or the Internet, Africa had griots, praise poets, and village elders, keepers of memory, masters of rhythm, and guardians of identity. They carried the continent's wisdom, laws, and legacies in living memory, passing them down through voice, performance, and ritual.

These oral archives are vast and profound, including mythology, family genealogies, songs of resistance, love stories, folktales, moral fables, and migration histories. The griot is not just a performer; they are an educator, historian, diplomat, and often a spiritual figure. In many communities, the storyteller's role is central to governance, cultural survival, and collective healing.

Yet modern life threatens this tradition. As younger generations move to urban centres, adopt digital lifestyles, and prioritise Western education, the oral traditions are fading. Without intervention, centuries of memory could vanish in a single lifetime.

We must preserve:

- ✧ Griot performances, songs, and praise poetry.
- ✧ Clan genealogies and lineage records passed down orally.
- ✧ Migration stories and origin tales of tribes and kingdoms.
- ✧ Myths, cosmologies, and spiritual teachings rooted in oral expression.
- ✧ Ceremonial speeches, royal praises, and ancestral invocations.

Preservation can take many forms, such as audio recordings, video documentation, stage performances, podcast storytelling, and transcription into books. African filmmakers, musicians, educators, and podcasters must become the new griots, bridging the oral tradition with the digital world, that when we honour our storytelling traditions, we don't just entertain, we educate, we heal, we inspire, and we remember who we are.

3. Traditional Knowledge and Innovation

Long before the age of globalisation, African communities had already developed highly sophisticated systems of knowledge rooted in observation, experimentation, and collective wisdom. These systems shaped how people lived, built, healed, governed, and sustained themselves. They were rarely written down but were deeply embedded in behaviour, passed down through generations, and adapted to local environments and needs.

What the world often celebrates today as "innovation" is, in many cases, what Africans have practised for centuries: rotational farming, sustainable architecture, herbal medicine, communal governance, and decentralised trade systems.

Yet these contributions are rarely recognised or credited because they have not been widely documented or validated through Western academic frameworks.

We must correct that narrative.

Africa's knowledge systems are not primitive; they are practical, contextual, and in many cases, ahead of their time. Preserving and reviving them is not about nostalgia; it is about survival, sustainability, and sovereignty.

We must preserve:

- ⬥ Indigenous agricultural techniques such as intercropping, terracing, seed saving, and seasonal rotation.
- ⬥ Traditional medicine and healing herbs, including local pharmacology and spiritual healing practices.
- ⬥ Sustainable housing models like mud-brick architecture, thatch insulation, and climate-responsive design.

- ✧ Rainwater harvesting, natural irrigation systems, and soil regeneration practices.
- ✧ Precolonial economic systems such as barter, trade routes, market days, communal resource sharing, and savings circles.
- ✧ Local approaches to conflict resolution, justice, and restorative healing.

These are not simply traditions; they are solutions to today's global challenges. Climate change, food insecurity, healthcare inequity, and urban overcrowding can all benefit from the wisdom embedded in Africa's traditional systems.

Documentation can take many forms:

- ✧ Video tutorials of elders demonstrating farming methods.
- ✧ Interviews with traditional healers and herbalists.
- ✧ Architectural plans and visual models of indigenous housing.
- ✧ Digital maps of ancient trade routes.
- ✧ Academic partnerships to test and validate traditional medicinal practices.

By preserving traditional knowledge, we do not reject progress; we enrich it. We ensure that future generations will not have to reinvent solutions their ancestors already mastered.

4. Spiritual and Religious Practices

Spirituality in Africa is not a separate compartment of life; it is the thread that weaves through every aspect of existence. From the veneration of ancestors in southern Africa to Ifá divination in Nigeria, spirituality is deeply integrated into African ethics, identity, medicine, agriculture, and governance. It shapes how communities understand illness and healing, justice and peace, birth and death, and the unseen forces that govern the world.

While many Africans today identify as Christian or Muslim, traditional beliefs and practices remain deeply influential, sometimes openly, sometimes subtly woven into personal rituals, language, music, and community values. Yet these spiritual systems are often misunderstood, dismissed, or erased, particularly by those who view them through colonial or strictly monotheistic lenses.

We must reclaim and preserve the spiritual frameworks that have guided our people for centuries, not as curiosities or relics, but as living systems of meaning, morality, and memory.

We must preserve:

- ✧ Ancestral rituals and ceremonies, including libations, prayers, and offerings to the departed.
- ✧ Sacred sites, shrines, and pilgrimage routes that serve as both spiritual and historical landmarks.
- ✧ Creation stories, cosmologies, pantheons of deities, and spiritual myths unique to different cultures.

- Rites of passage such as naming ceremonies, puberty rituals, initiation, marriage customs, and funeral traditions.
- Indigenous priesthoods, diviners, healers, and the spiritual teachings they safeguard.

Preservation methods can include:

- Recording oral testimonies from spiritual leaders and elders.
- Mapping and documenting sacred spaces before they are encroached upon or destroyed.
- Filming rituals and ceremonies with consent from custodians and communities.
- Archiving spiritual music, chants, and dance forms.
- Translating and publishing spiritual texts and oral teachings.

This is not simply about spirituality; it is about sovereignty. When we understand and preserve our spiritual systems, we reclaim the dignity and agency that colonisation sought to strip away. We affirm that African ways of knowing the divine are valid, rich, and worthy of transmission and preservation. To truly know Africa, we must understand how it prays, meditates, heals, and connects to the unseen.

5. Cultural Expressions: Music, Dance, and Art

Africa doesn't just make music; it *is* music. From the steady heartbeat of the djembe to the sacred hum of chants sung during initiation rites, African cultural expressions are not merely entertainment; they are archives of our spirit, history, resistance, and hope. They carry coded messages, ancestral memory, and communal identity across generations and geographies.

Our music gave birth to the blues, sung by enslaved Africans on plantations, evolved into jazz in Harlem, travelled through Kingston as reggae, and re-emerged as Afrobeat and Amapiano, pulsing on global stages. Nevertheless, long before these genres were exported and commercialised, they were tools of storytelling, spiritual warfare, healing, and celebration in the village square.

Our dances are not just movements; they are maps. Each step in a ceremonial dance, from the Maasai adumu to the Ivorian Zaouli, is a remembrance of migration, a marker of spiritual transition, and a performance of identity. Dance communicates what words cannot, whether in weddings, harvests, funerals, or rites of passage.

Our art, both sacred and daily, speaks across mediums in the patterns of Kente cloth, in the scarification on cheeks and shoulders, in the symbols etched onto calabashes or painted on walls. African textiles, masks, beads, body paint, and murals have always carried meaning, marking tribe, status, role, and spiritual purpose. These expressions were never merely decorative. They were functional, encoded systems of knowledge, power, and connection.

Yet today, much of our heritage is under threat from commercialisation and foreign appropriation, leading to the loss of oral custodians and digital erasure. As African museums remain empty while our artefacts sit in European vaults, we must ask: Who is curating our creativity? Who is telling our story?

To preserve the soul of African expression for future generations and ensure our contributions remain visible in the age of AI and cultural algorithms, we must document and digitise our creative legacy.

Preserve:

- ⟡ Traditional instruments (like the kora, balafon, mbira) and their playing techniques.
- ⟡ Ceremonial dances, their meanings, contexts, and attire.
- ⟡ Symbolism in visual arts, murals, beadwork, and textiles.
- ⟡ Tribal markings, body art, hairstyles, and their social meanings.
- ⟡ Songs, chants, and stories passed through generations.
- ⟡ The philosophies behind performance, not just the performance itself.

Africa is not a continent of silence. It is a symphony of expression. We must write it down, record it, code it, and pass it on.

6. Fashion and Textile Heritage

In Africa, fashion is not just what we wear, it is who we are. It is history woven into cloth, identity stitched into seams, and spirituality dyed into colour. Every thread tells a story.

From the bold geometry of Kente cloth in Ghana, worn by kings and queens to declare power and wisdom, to the rich indigo fabrics of Mali's bogolanfini (mud cloth), used to mark status, fertility, and spiritual protection, African textiles have always been a language of their own.

In Uganda, bark cloth, made from the inner bark of the mutuba tree, connects the Baganda people to their ancestors and is still worn during royal and funeral rites as an unbroken thread through centuries of change.

These textiles are not just beautiful; they are intentional. The colours worn at weddings, funerals, or coronations aren't chosen for fashion; they reflect beliefs, seasons, life stages, and moral values. Red may symbolise sacrifice; white, purity or mourning; gold, wealth and divinity.

Traditional African fashion also celebrates form and function. Beadwork, particularly among the Maasai and Zulu, conveys age, marital status, and social rank. Jewellery, from bronze bangles to cowrie-studded belts, is more than an ornament; it is economic currency, spiritual armour, and a cultural archive. Even hairstyles were once detailed tribal signatures used to identify community, readiness for marriage, or warrior status.

Yet today, the global fashion industry often imitates without acknowledging. African prints are mass-produced in foreign factories, our designs repackaged without credit, and our sacred garments reduced to seasonal trends. The danger isn't just theft. It's erasure. As elders pass without passing down their craft, and youth trade bark cloth for denim, we risk losing a deeply coded heritage.

If we do not document, protect, and innovate around our own fashion legacy, we will find ourselves wearing history written by others.

Preserve:

- ✧ Traditional weaving, spinning, and dyeing techniques (tie-dye, mud cloth, loom weaving).
- ✧ The meaning behind patterns, shapes, and colour symbolism across regions.
- ✧ Ceremonial and everyday attire, who wore what, when, and why.
- ✧ Beadwork patterns, jewellery making, body adornment, and the stories they hold.
- ✧ Oral traditions tied to dress (e.g., when to wear mourning cloth or initiation garments).
- ✧ Fashion as a living archive of African kingdoms, communities, and belief systems.

Fashion in Africa is not fast; it is forever. Let us document it before it fades into imitation.

7. Food and Culinary Traditions

Food in Africa is more than nourishment; it is memory, ceremony, and identity served on a plate. It is the laughter around a shared pot, the aroma that signals homecoming, the recipe that bridges generations. To eat in Africa is to participate in culture.

Across the continent, cuisine is as diverse as its people: injera in Ethiopia, matoke in Uganda, jollof rice in West

Africa, nyama choma in Kenya, fufu in Ghana and Nigeria, and couscous in North Africa. Each dish carries the spirit of a people, shaped by geography, migration, colonial history, and spiritual beliefs.

Beyond ingredients lies meaning in many cultures, showing how food is grown, prepared, served, and eaten reflects values and worldviews. Who cooks? Who eats first? What is shared or saved for guests or ancestors? These are codes of respect and order, not just customs.

Preparation methods like slow wood-fire cooking, mortar pounding, fermentation, smoking, sun-drying, and clay-pot steaming are not only efficient and sustainable, but they also preserve nutrients, flavour, and heritage. Communal eating, often with hands from one bowl, reflects the African philosophy of Ubuntu: "I am because we are."

Food also marks sacred moments. Harvest festivals celebrate abundance and express gratitude to ancestors. Initiation and marriage ceremonies feature specific dishes tied to rites of passage. Even mourning comes with its own culinary symbols.

Yet as fast-food chains replace local vendors, and imported grains push aside indigenous crops, much is being lost. Recipes once passed down by storytelling or apprenticeship risk extinction. Indigenous superfoods sorghum, teff, millet, moringa, baobab, and fonio are undervalued or forgotten in favour of Western alternatives, despite being healthier and more ecologically suited.

Without documentation, African food traditions will be misrepresented, misappropriated, or vanish altogether. Who will write our cookbooks not just with ingredients, but with meaning?

Preserve:

- Generational recipes, cooking stories, and community food roles.
- Indigenous preparation methods like open-fire, clay pot, fermentation, and drying.
- Culinary customs tied to birth, initiation, marriage, harvest, and death.
- Native crops, herbs, spices, and their cultural and medicinal meanings.
- Cooking songs, taboos, and proverbs shared during food preparation.
- Traditional tools and vessels from grinding stones to banana-leaf wraps.

Food is our earliest language of love, land, and lineage. If we don't record it, future generations will inherit only empty plates.

8. Architecture and Land Use

In Africa, architecture has never been about bricks alone. It has always been about balance. Balance with nature, with ancestors, with the seasons, and with spirit. Long before the modern idea of green building, African architecture practiced environmental harmony, sustainability, and community-centred design.

Vernacular architecture, whether the earthen homes of the Sahel, the circular rondavels of Southern Africa, the stilted water villages in Benin, or the stone structures of the Dogon in Mali, was shaped not by ego but by ecology. Materials were locally sourced: mud, thatch, timber, reeds, and volcanic stone. Designs took into account wind flow, solar exposure, rainwater collection, and cultural norms.

Architecture was not only functional but symbolic. The layout of a home could reflect cosmology; the entrance, a rite; the hearth, a portal. In Buganda, for example, the royal palace (Lubiri) and traditional homes carried meaning in how they were built, who could enter, and how space was arranged to reflect respect and rank. Walls were not just boundaries. They were social scripts.

Across the continent, sacred spaces, groves, shrines, pyramids, temples, and ancestral graves were woven into the land, not imposed upon it. These were places of ritual, memory, and spiritual governance. Architecture served not just the physical needs of life but also the metaphysical continuity of the community.

Ancient African cities such as Timbuktu, Great Zimbabwe, Lalibela, and Carthage show that African urban planning predated colonial layouts by centuries. These cities had marketplaces, educational centres, spiritual quarters, irrigation systems, and sophisticated governance structures. Their design emphasised communal access, trade, sustainability, and coexistence with nature.

Land use itself was communal, guided by tradition and elders. Land was not owned it was entrusted. It was a living entity to be respected, inherited with responsibility, and shared for the benefit of all. Colonialism disrupted this balance, imposing rigid boundaries, private titles, and extractive exploitation, leading to land conflicts and cultural erosion that still plague Africa today.

Today, African cities are expanding rapidly but often following models that ignore our indigenous wisdom. Glass towers replace clay homes. Gated communities replace communal compounds. If we fail to preserve and modernise our own design principles, we risk living in borrowed spaces that do not reflect who we are.

We must preserve:

- ✧ Vernacular architecture: designs, materials, and the meanings behind indigenous building styles.
- ✧ Sacred spaces: temples, shrines, palaces, spiritual forests, and their community roles.
- ✧ Ancient urban planning: the blueprints of cities like Timbuktu, Mapungubwe, Axum, and Djenné.
- ✧ Indigenous land-use systems: communal ownership, land rituals, and inheritance customs.
- ✧ Traditional architecture linked to status, gender roles, and spiritual protection.
- ✧ Sustainable design principles rooted in African traditions.

Africa built before it borrowed. Let us record and revive our architectural genius before it is bulldozed.

9. Social Structures and Governance

Before colonial borders were established and constitutions were drafted in European languages, Africa governed itself wisely, dynamically, and with deep respect for human life, community, and the spiritual world. Precolonial African societies had governance systems rooted in consensus, elder wisdom, accountability, and balance, not simply in power.

Across the continent, councils of elders settled disputes, upheld customs, and served as living archives of law and history. These councils operated with memory and moral authority, often without written texts, yet with a clarity and fairness that kept generations in order. Their decisions were guided by principles of ubuntu (humanity toward others), ma'at (truth and balance), and other culturally grounded philosophies.

Many societies used age-grade systems, where generational cohorts determined roles, duties, and leadership. In the Igbo, Maasai, and Oromo traditions, individuals progressed through ranks with age and achievement, not merely wealth or inheritance. This ensured that leadership was earned through experience and service, not imposed by force or manipulated by politics.

Chieftaincy systems were not just about power. They were about protection, stewardship, and continuity. Whether it was the Kabaka of Buganda, the Oba of Benin, the Zulu iNkosi, or the Tuareg amenokal, traditional leaders were custodians of land, culture, and spirituality. Their titles carried sacred weight, and their authority was often balanced by councils or religious advisors, preventing centralised absolutism.

African societies also had indigenous legal codes and justice systems. Conflict resolution was often restorative rather than punitive, focusing on healing, restitution, and reintegration rather than imprisonment or exile. Disputes over land, marriage, or theft were resolved through public gatherings, where testimony, oaths, and symbolic acts were used, often invoking the land, ancestors, or community rituals.

In many places, governance was decentralised, organised through clans, lineages, or village assemblies. Decisions required consensus, not just command. Roles were distributed among spiritual leaders, warriors, rainmakers, healers, and storytellers, all of whom contributed to a governance ecosystem that valued balance over domination.

Yet much of this knowledge is fading or has been distorted by colonial administration, political manipulation, and the disconnection from oral sources. Modern states have often imported foreign systems that clash with indigenous realities. What was once alive in practice is now locked in memory if remembered at all.

If we are to build future governance rooted in justice and dignity, we must revisit the blueprints that held us together before conquest.

We must preserve:

- ✧ Traditional conflict resolution mechanisms (e.g., Gacaca courts in Rwanda, Mato Oput in Acholi culture).

- ⬥ Chieftaincy systems, roles, titles, rituals, and their spiritual/social functions.
- ⬥ Age-grade structures and lineage-based governance models.
- ⬥ Legal codes passed through oral tradition, symbolic oaths, and ritual practices.
- ⬥ Community organisation systems (e.g., village assemblies, clan councils, guild structures).
- ⬥ Ethical frameworks that guided leadership accountability to people, land, and spirit.

Africa didn't lack governance; it had governance rooted in values, relationships, and balance. Let us document it before the silence becomes permanent.

10. Historical Events and Resistance Movements

History is not neutral; those with the power to document write it. And for too long, Africa's history has been written by outsiders who highlighted conquest and ignored courage, who recorded exploitation but erased resistance.

Yet Africa did not accept its fate in silence. From the shores of Senegal to the highlands of Ethiopia, the continent rose, fought, negotiated, endured, and dreamed. Even post-independence milestones, such as the Pan-African movement, the birth of the African Union, the rise of African statesmen and women, economic revolts, and constitutional reforms, must be documented. The political evolution of countries like Ghana, Tanzania, Rwanda, and South Africa holds valuable lessons for future leaders, yet these milestones are often overlooked, relegated to academic archives or relegated to foreign documentaries.

History must not just be remembered; it must be owned. To own it, we must write it, preserve it, teach it, and pass it on.

We must preserve:

- ⟡ Stories of anti-colonial resistance: revolts, liberation wars, secret societies, and spiritual uprisings.
- ⟡ Oral histories of migrations, inter-tribal alliances, and key battles (e.g., Adwa, Isandlwana, Maji Maji).
- ⟡ Biographies of heroic African figures, both well-known and unsung, community leaders.
- ⟡ Post-independence turning points: constitutional changes, revolutions, coups, and peace processes.
- ⟡ Pan-African movements, intellectual resistance, and African contributions to global freedom struggles.
- ⟡ Community memory: songs, poems, grave sites, monuments, and rituals that recall historical truth.

Africa's history didn't begin with colonisation, and it didn't end at independence. We are the authors of revolutions, not just their victims. If we don't write it down, our descendants will be taught that we were passive when, in truth, we were powerful.

11. Philosophies, Values, and Ethics

Before the arrival of foreign religions and legal systems, Africa already had a moral compass. Our ancestors lived by philosophies rooted in harmony, dignity, reciprocity, and responsibility. These were not just abstract ideas, they were embodied truths, passed down in proverbs, practised in rituals, and enforced through communal living.

Ubuntu in Southern Africa teaches: "I am because we are." It is a value system that prioritises interdependence, compassion, and mutual respect. **Harambee** in Kenya calls for pulling together, reminding communities that no success is achieved in isolation. **Sankofa** in Ghana reminds us to return and fetch what we've forgotten, because our past is not behind us, it is the root of our future.

These are not just slogans, they are systems of ethics embedded into how people marry, raise children, resolve conflict, bury the dead, and lead communities. African societies were governed by codes of conduct that emphasised the importance of upholding truth, hospitality, respect for elders, generosity, and care for the vulnerable.

Taboos weren't just superstitions; they were often ecological or moral guidelines passed down through oral law. Oaths and covenants were sacred, often sealed before ancestors or nature spirits, and breaking them came with serious spiritual and social consequences.

Children weren't raised by parents alone; they belonged to the entire community. Communal child-rearing taught shared responsibility, generational continuity, and identity formation from an early age. Any elder could correct a child who misbehaved. In this way, morality wasn't individualistic; it was communal, nurtured and enforced through a living network of relationships.

Ceremonial rituals around birth, naming, initiation, marriage, and death were not just traditions, they were theological frameworks. They carried spiritual significance and ensured smooth transitions between stages of life. From the pouring of libation at weddings to the shaving of heads during mourning, these practices reminded us that life is sacred, cyclical, and shared.

As modern life erodes communal bonds and external cultures reshape our worldview, many of these philosophies risk fading into nostalgia or misinterpretation. But these are not dead ideas, they are blueprints for a humane and just society.

We must preserve:

- ✧ Proverbs, idioms, and maxims that carry generational wisdom.
- ✧ Ethical codes: hospitality laws, truth-telling customs, taboos, and honour systems.
- ✧ Communal child-rearing models: roles of aunties, uncles, elders, and community rites.
- ✧ Rituals marking key life events: birth naming, puberty initiation, marriage traditions, and funeral rites.
- ✧ Indigenous moral teachings embedded in songs, stories, and daily practices.

◆ Theologies of nature, ancestors, and human purpose rooted in African cosmologies.

Africa's wisdom is not just intellectual it is embodied. It is time we document these truths, not just for academia, but for our survival.

12. Diaspora Stories and Contributions

Africa is not bound by geography, it is a spirit, a memory, and a people scattered yet connected across oceans and centuries. Our story does not end at the shores of the continent; it stretches into Brazil, Haiti, Cuba, Jamaica, Trinidad, the United States, the United Kingdom, France, and beyond. From the trauma of displacement to the triumph of cultural reinvention, the African diaspora holds a vital chapter of our collective identity.

The transatlantic slave trade was not just a historical atrocity. It was a rupture. Families were torn apart, languages silenced, and spiritual systems outlawed. But even in bondage, Africans resisted. They preserved identity in code through drumbeats, braids, folktales, and food. Rebellions erupted in maroon communities and plantations; spiritual practices like Vodun, Santería, and Candomblé rose from suppressed African belief systems.

Out of forced migration came diasporic cultural evolution: jazz, blues, gospel, samba, hip-hop, capoeira, spoken word, and soul food. These were not just adaptations, they were acts of resistance, reinvention, and reclamation. They prove that Africa lives wherever its people do.

The diaspora also birthed Black intellectual thought, from W.E.B. Du Bois to Frantz Fanon, Aimé Césaire to Audre Lorde, James Baldwin to bell hooks. These thinkers challenged global systems of racism, colonialism, and capitalism. They redefined African identity in exile and built bridges back to the continent through literature, politics, and revolution.

Transcontinental movements such as Pan-Africanism, Rastafarianism, the Civil Rights Movement, Negritude, and Black Lives Matter have all been fuelled by the African diaspora's desire not only to survive but to define freedom on their own terms. The diaspora's contributions to Africa include financial remittances, philosophy, art, spirituality, and revolution.

To publish Africa means publishing the diaspora too its pain, pride, and power.

We must preserve:

- ✧ Narratives of the transatlantic slave trade and African resistance in the Americas.
- ✧ Diasporic expressions of African spirituality, music, language, and culinary arts.
- ✧ Writings, speeches, and philosophies of Black thought leaders.
- ✧ Pan-African political movements, solidarity campaigns, and cross-border activism.
- ✧ Identity struggles and triumphs of second and third-generation diaspora youth.
- ✧ Reconnection efforts return journeys, DNA tracing, dual citizenship, and cultural restoration.

The Cost of Not Preserving

When we fail to preserve these stories, we lose facts plus ourselves. Every undocumented ritual, unrecorded elder, extinct dialect, or misrepresented belief chips away at our cultural DNA. And in an age where written records shape global algorithms, artificial intelligence, and curriculum design, what is not documented does not exist.

This silence leaves us vulnerable to cultural colonisation, where our identity is replaced with borrowed narratives; to economic exploitation, where our ideas are stolen and resold to us; and to spiritual confusion, where younger generations no longer know who they are or where they come from.

Preservation is not just about pride; it is about protection.

Towards a Preservation Agenda

Preservation is not a nostalgic luxury; it is a strategic and urgent need. It must be intentional, systematic, and sustained. Whether you are a government official, an artist, an elder, a teacher, or a youth, this is your call to action.

To move forward, we must:

- **Map our cultural assets** – from language speakers to sacred sites, festivals to foodways. Every community has a living inventory of heritage that must be identified before it disappears.

- ➤ **Engage elders and custodians** – record oral histories, songs, rituals, and community laws before the knowledge bearers are gone.
- ➤ **Digitise fragile materials** – transcribe, translate, scan, and upload what can be saved to ensure it survives both time and technology shifts.
- ➤ **Train the youth** – equip a new generation of preservationists, archivists, translators, and storytellers to continue the work.
- ➤ **Create accessible archives** – build community libraries, mobile apps, virtual museums, and open databases where Africans everywhere can access and contribute to their own history.
- ➤ **Protect intellectual property** – ensure that African traditions, innovations, and symbols are not exploited without consent or fair compensation.

Preservation must become a lifestyle, a daily act of remembering, recording, and respecting who we are. It is not something we do once; it is something we become.

Final Call: Publishing Africa, Preserving Ourselves

This chapter is your checklist. This book is your call. As we rise in numbers, influence, and technological power, we must ensure that we do not rise as strangers to our own story.

We must publish our languages before they vanish into silence.

We must publish our land before it is stolen or redefined.

We must publish our legends before others rewrite them.

We must publish our philosophies so our values endure.

We must publish our food so our taste of home is never lost.

We must publish our fashion so that our heritage is worn with pride.

We must publish our pain because our struggles hold lessons for the world.

We must publish our possibilities because our future deserves to be imagined by us, not for us.

Preservation is not simply about holding on to the past; it is about protecting the foundations upon which our future will stand. Without deliberate documentation, we will continue to be defined by borrowed narratives, diminished by incomplete histories, and displaced in the digital archives that shape tomorrow's world.

Africa must move from being a subject in someone else's archive to being the author of its own record.

The tools are in our hands. The urgency is in our time. The responsibility is ours.

Let us document with discipline, publish with purpose, and preserve with pride, for in doing so, we ensure that Africa is not just remembered, but remembered rightly.

When we publish Africa, we preserve ourselves. And in preserving ourselves, we shape the destiny of generations yet unborn.

CHAPTER FOUR

IF WE DON'T PUBLISH, WE PERISH

"If it's not written, it never happened. If it's not documented, it doesn't exist."

—**Geoffrey Semaganda**

Africa is the cradle of humanity. Our rivers have fed kingdoms, our soil has grown civilisations, and our spirit has endured empires. From Egypt to Axum, from the Kingdom of Kush to Great Zimbabwe, from the oral laws of the Ashanti to the star-mapping Dogon, Africa has always been a continent of brilliance.

But today, existence is no longer determined by history, it is measured by data. In the digital age, visibility defines legitimacy. What is not documented is invisible. What is not searchable is forgettable. What is not digitised may as well not exist.

And so, despite our undeniable contributions to the human story, Africa is being erased not by violence, but by silence.

The critical consequences of non-documentation are that if we fail to publish our ideas, our history, our philosophies, and our innovations, we will not only be excluded from global systems but also become ghosts in the age of machines.

The Age of Artificial Intelligence: Content Is King

We are living through the most transformative technological shift since the Industrial Revolution. Artificial Intelligence (AI) is not coming, it is already here. It powers how we learn, shop, govern, bank, heal, build, and connect. From Siri to ChatGPT, from YouTube algorithms to medical diagnostic systems, AI is shaping reality, and it is doing so based on what has already been written.

AI models are trained on massive volumes of existing content: books, academic papers, websites, news articles, podcasts, social media, legal documents, and historical records. These models do not have opinions; they have data. And data comes from what is available. If your culture hasn't been written down, published, or digitised, it will not be reflected.

Consider this: Africa accounts for over 20% of the world's population, yet it contributes less than 2% of global digital content (UNESCO, 2021). That means 98% of the content feeding AI systems does not represent African knowledge, voices, or values.

The consequences are profound and dangerous.

Underrepresentation in AI Outputs

AI tools frequently generate answers that ignore or distort African realities. From geography to history, many African countries are misrepresented or completely omitted.

Ask a language model about African philosophies, and you may get a handful of shallow references. Search for African medicinal knowledge, and Western summaries dominate. In voice recognition tools, African accents are often misunderstood or unsupported.

Cultural and Identity Bias

Artificial intelligence is increasingly embedded in hiring decisions, education platforms, healthcare diagnostics, business analytics, law enforcement, online matchmaking, and content moderation. If African languages, ethics, proverbs, and customs are absent from the data that trains these systems, our communities will be misjudged, mistreated, or ignored. We risk a future in which machines do not recognise us, understand us, or serve us.

Lost Influence in Global Solutions

Africa faces unique challenges, including climate crises, informal economies, community-based healthcare, and multilingual societies. Yet AI tools being deployed to "solve" these problems are often built without African input or data. The result is technological colonialism solutions imposed, not grown from within.

Digital Neo-Colonialism

When foreign platforms dominate the tools, the data, and the content, Africa is not just underrepresented, we are owned. Our knowledge is scraped and sold back to us. Our silence becomes their algorithmic power.

The new literacy of this age is simple: publish or perish. Content is capital. Whoever controls the data controls the direction of the world. Publishing African knowledge is no longer just cultural preservation, it is a geopolitical strategy. Documentation is not about nostalgia; it is about negotiating power. Writing down our truth is not just for memory; it is for survival.

Just as land was once colonised and extracted, our minds, data, and stories are now at risk of digital exploitation. If we do not tell our story, machines will tell it for us, and they will get it wrong.

The good news? We are not helpless. Africa has millions of untold stories, thousands of languages, countless proverbs, philosophies, and innovations waiting to be recorded. We have the talent, the tools, and the time if we start now.

The question is not whether Africa has something to say. The question is: will we write it down before it's too late?

The Danger of a One-Sided Story

"The problem with stereotypes is not that they are untrue, but that they are incomplete."
— Chimamanda Ngozi Adichie
Nigerian author Chimamanda Ngozi Adichie sounded the global alarm when she spoke about "the danger of a single story." For Africa, that danger has become a full-blown crisis.

The dominant narratives about Africa that circulate globally follow the same tired template: poverty, disease, corruption, and conflict. These are the stories most documented, most published, most quoted, and most consumed. They are not all lies, but they are incomplete, and an incomplete story is a distorted truth.

When the only content available about Africa focuses on despair, the world begins to define us by our deficits, not our depth. And stories shape systems.

Outsiders who tell our story, whether from boardrooms, media desks, NGO offices, or development agencies, do so with limited historical context, often with political or commercial agendas, and rarely with understanding, instead relying on translation rather than transformation.

These narratives shape aid strategies that assume Africans are helpless, tourism campaigns that exoticize wildlife while ignoring vibrant urban life, investment decisions where risk is exaggerated and opportunity underestimated, immigration policies that treat African passports as red flags, and media representation that frames us as a problem to be solved rather than a partner to be respected.

Worse, we begin to internalise these incomplete stories. Our youth start to believe Africa is cursed. Our professionals chase validation abroad. Our artists feel pressure to write pain instead of power because struggle sells.

I still travel to global conferences, airports, and hotels and feel like a stranger to those who look at me. Not because I don't know who I am, but because they don't. They are not seeing me; they are seeing the story someone else told them about where I'm from. This is what happens when we don't write ourselves into the record. Silence is not neutral. Silence is submission. When we do not speak, others speak on our behalf. When we do not publish, others publish about us. When we are misrepresented, we are misunderstood. And when we are misunderstood, we are mistreated.

Publishing Africa is a cultural project and a justice mission. We are not simply trying to tell our side of the story. We are restoring the fullness of who we are.

If We Don't Document, We Can't Educate

Education is not just about passing exams; it is about passing on identity. It is about giving children the confidence to know who they are, where they come from, and what they carry. That confidence is rooted in content.

Suppose the textbooks, storybooks, school libraries, and curricula that African children encounter are written by foreign authors, built on foreign values, and focused on foreign heroes. In that case, the child is silently taught that their own culture is secondary. They may become literate but not liberated. They may memorise but not recognise themselves.

Education divorced from cultural content is a quiet form of alienation. And for many African children today, this is their daily classroom experience: they read about the Eiffel Tower, but not the Great Mosque of Djenné; they can name Aristotle, but not Imhotep or Nana Asma'u; they recite Shakespeare, but have never encountered Okot p'Bitek (Uganda), Wole Soyinka

(Nigeria), or Ngũgĩ wa Thiong'o (Kenya); they learn about the Amazon rainforest, but not the Congo Basin or the Sahel's adaptation systems.

This absence is not only a missed opportunity but also a form of miseducation.

Without African content, inventors, scientists, and philosophers are erased from imagination. Indigenous knowledge systems in medicine, agriculture, architecture, and governance are replaced with unsuitable models. African languages are dismissed as obstacles rather than intellectual tools. Traditional wisdom is lost or trivialised.

Education becomes a vehicle of dependency, not dignity. But publishing is education. Books are more than ink on paper; they are vessels of cultural transfer. They carry the stories, values, innovations, and wisdom of a people across time.

When we do not publish, we lose continuity. If we don't document our knowledge, we cannot teach it. If we cannot teach it, we cannot build upon it. And if we cannot build upon it, we stagnate while the world moves on.

A people without self-knowledge is a people without direction. A nation that cannot educate its own with its own content is still being colonised quietly, every day, in its classrooms.

This is why publishing is not an artistic luxury. It is an educational emergency.

If We Don't Publish, We Lose Economic Opportunity

Publishing is not just cultural, it is commercial. It is the engine behind global industries that generate influence, revenue, and sustainable jobs. From the books we read to the shows we stream, the podcasts we binge, to the online courses we enrol in, content is currency.

Yet in this trillion-dollar global content economy, Africa's share remains painfully small. Not because we lack stories, talent, or creativity, but because we lack systems to document, protect, and monetise what we already have in abundance. We consume more than we produce. We import more stories than we export. We inspire global trends yet often own none of the platforms that profit from our voice.

When we fail to publish our stories, wisdom, innovations, and cultural expressions, we miss out on billions in intellectual property revenue. We allow outsiders to monetise our heritage through books, courses, tourism, films, and museum exhibits.

Local creative authors, animators, screenwriters, researchers, and designers are underpaid, undervalued, and often forced to look abroad for recognition and income. Our languages, proverbs, designs, and rituals are copyrighted by non-African companies and sold back to us with no benefit to the communities of origin.

But imagine the alternative. What if every African village had its legends published? Every tribe had its dances documented and digitised? Every elder had their wisdom archived and turned into micro-courses? Every local language has stories available on children's apps, YouTube, and audiobooks?

This would unleash a wave of new industries. Cultural and creative economies would flourish through cultural tourism driven by documented heritage sites, festivals, and ancestral journeys; heritage merchandise such as clothing, artwork, musical instruments, books, and crafts based on real cultural assets; streaming platforms for African films, podcasts, and oral history; and book publishing for global education systems seeking diverse, authentic content.

Education and knowledge economies would also expand curriculum development rooted in African philosophy, science, leadership, and languages; online learning academies teaching everything from drumming and beadwork to African economics and environmental knowledge; digital publishing jobs for editors, illustrators, translators, and audio technicians; and local AI data hubs training future tech models on African content rather than Western-only datasets.

The economic opportunity is massive. But it starts with documentation. You cannot monetise what is not published. You cannot protect what is not archived. You cannot scale what has not been written down.

Publishing Africa is not a charity; it is an untapped economic engine. It is a road to job creation, youth empowerment, diaspora investment, and global visibility. And just like oil, gold, and cocoa, our stories are a resource. But unlike those, they are renewable.

If We Don't Publish, We Forget Ourselves

Memory is not a luxury. It is survival. To be human is to remember. To be a people is to preserve memory across generations. And the tool we use to preserve that memory is documentation.

When we publish, we anchor our identity. We build continuity between the past, the present, and the future. But when we fail to document who we are, what we believe, and how we live, we begin to vanish from our own minds.

Without records, lineages are lost, and children no longer know the names or totems of their ancestors. Sacred sites are erased, turned into construction zones, or forgotten wastelands. Languages go extinct with every funeral; another dialect dies quietly. Lessons from past conflicts are forgotten, so we repeat the same divisions. Rituals become confused, diluted, or commercialised, reduced to photo ops instead of sacred transitions.

Cultural loss is not always loud. Sometimes it is subtle: a story not told, a custom not practised, a proverb forgotten. However, the damage remains the same; we begin to lose ourselves.

When a generation of elders dies without recording their wisdom, what follows is not just silence, it is cultural amnesia. What took a thousand years to develop a healing practice, a moral code, a clan structure, and a naming ceremony can vanish in a decade of neglect.

A continent that does not preserve its memory cannot build continuity. It will constantly reinvent the wheel, borrow from others, and second-guess itself. It will look outward for inspiration because it no longer remembers its own greatness.

Nations must be rooted in their stories if they are to grow with clarity and pride. Publishing through books, audio, film, or digital archives is the tool that makes remembrance possible. This is not about glorifying the past. It is about remembering enough of who we are to shape who we must become.

Because if we don't publish, we forget. And when we forget, we fracture.

And when we fracture, we are easier to manipulate, marginalise, or erase.

Let us be a generation that interrupts that cycle. Let us write it down. Record it. Translate it. Protect it. Let us preserve Africa before we forget how.

The Geopolitics of Knowledge

There is a quiet war unfolding not over land, oil, or gold, but over influence. It is a race to control the world's narratives, worldviews, and imagination. This is the geopolitics of knowledge, and right now, Africa is losing.

The battlefield is not only in parliaments or ports it is in books and textbooks, documentaries and media outlets, search engines and streaming platforms, school curricula and university libraries, algorithms, databases, and AI training sets.

The nations and institutions that dominate content today will shape the global conscience tomorrow. They will decide what is remembered, what is respected, and what is rewarded.

The U.S. dominates entertainment, Hollywood, Netflix, YouTube, and social media. China dominates infrastructure and digital tools. Europe dominates academic publishing. But who dominates the story of Africa? Too often, the answer is not us.

Even when our stories are told, they are filtered through foreign editors, foreign grants, and foreign expectations. Even when our knowledge is used, it is extracted, repackaged, and copyrighted elsewhere. Even when our images go global, the narrative rights and revenue stay outside the continent.

This is not just about representation. It is about sovereignty. If we do not take control of our intellectual property, our historical narratives, and our philosophical frameworks, others will. And they will license them back to us in books, documentaries, apps, tourism, and software reflecting their perspective, not ours.

This is already happening. African designs are trademarked abroad. African languages are used in tech without consent or compensation. African history is taught internationally with little input from African scholars. African characters appear in films and video games, but are rarely written by Africans themselves.

This is digital colonialism, not with force, but with omission and outsourcing. The real power today lies not just in land or military, but in the mind. The future belongs to those who shape how people think, feel, dream, vote, and build. And that shaping begins with the written word.

If Africa does not invest in publishing, documentation, translation, and narrative control, we will remain consumers in a world where creators determine value. To win the future, we must write ourselves into it not for pity, not for permission, but for power.

The Youth Will Inherit What We Publish

Africa's greatest resource is not buried underground. It is walking, talking, dreaming, and tweeting. Over 65% of Africa's population is under the age of twenty-five. We are not just a young continent; we are a rising continent.

But what will we pass down to the next generation? Will we hand them empty libraries, missing archives, and languages they never learned to read? Or will we give them blueprints of identity, maps of memory, and stories of power they can build on?

Suppose we do not publish for our youth. In that case, they will grow up disoriented, seeking models of success in foreign cultures, inheriting tools that solve Western problems but not African ones, and treating their own traditions as obsolete instead of innovative.

But if we do publish for them, they will rise with confidence rooted in heritage. They will turn screens into storytelling platforms, voices into vessels of ancestral wisdom, and ideas into industries. They will animate folktales, record podcasts in local dialects, and train AI on African proverbs. They will take what we preserve and propel it into the future.

Publishing is not just preservation. It is preparation. A documented culture is an armed culture, not with violence but with vision. And vision is what our youth need most, not just to escape poverty, but to design prosperity in their own image. They will inherit whatever we choose to publish or fail to publish. If we write it, they will remember it. If we digitise it, they will distribute it. If we elevate it, they will evolve it.

Let us not leave them searching for themselves in someone else's story. Let us give them Africa documented, dignified, and daring.

If We Don't Publish, We Perish Politically

Politics is not just about power. It is about ideas made permanent. And the primary vehicle of permanence is the written word.

Every constitution begins as a document. Every rights movement starts with a manifesto. Every law is encoded. Every revolution remembered. If we do not publish our political thought, we do not exist in the realm of political influence.

When African leaders, thinkers, activists, and institutions fail to document their ideologies and governance models, our systems remain reactive instead of visionary. We inherit foreign policies often incompatible with African realities. Our youth study Western philosophers but know little about our own. We remain perpetual students in global diplomacy rather than authors of our own doctrine.

This has consequences. African democracy is often measured by imported standards, not indigenous definitions of consensus or justice. Grassroots movements lose momentum because their ideas are never crystallised into documents. The memory of political trailblazers, women freedom fighters, anti-colonial strategists, and rural mobilizers is lost because no memoirs were written, and no lessons were archived.

Without documentation, African political thought is reduced to headlines and hashtags, not legacy. What we need is a renaissance of African political publishing: manifestos grounded in Pan-African values, policy documents rooted in African economic philosophies, memoirs of freedom fighters, and constitutional comment

Faith, Family, and the Soul of Africa

Faith in Africa is not just personal. It is communal, generational, and sacred. From the chants of ancient temples to the whispered prayers of grandmothers, our spiritual identity is a living archive of resilience, guidance, and hope. Yet today, much of that archive is under threat, not because the faith has weakened but because it is undocumented.

Walk into churches, mosques, and shrines across the continent, some with tens of thousands of followers, and you will often find no written doctrine, no published testimonies, no preserved founding story. A spiritual revival is happening across Africa, but it risks being forgotten the moment its founders pass on.

Ask many Africans about their ancestry, and most can only trace back one or two generations. Names, migrations, marriages, and legacies are buried in memory, not in print. Indigenous belief systems dismissed as "pagan" or erased hold centuries of wisdom on justice, community, healing, and nature. Yet they are fading because we have not documented them.

By failing to publish, we allow others to define our faith, reduce our families to footnotes, and dilute sacred knowledge. We risk having our spiritual truths reinterpreted without our consent.

It is time to reclaim that power. Faith-based institutions must rise not only to preach, but to publish. Sermons must become books. Testimonies must become documentaries. Oral traditions must be transcribed. Family trees must be drawn, archived, and passed down like sacred scrolls.

Publishing is not just preservation; it is protection. It is how we guard our truth and pass on our soul.

The Time to Publish Is Now

We are not waiting for the future. We are already standing in it. Africa is no longer a continent "awaiting development." We are a global force, young, resourceful, creative, and spiritually rooted. But in the age of acceleration, where change is measured in algorithms, not generations, those who fail to document will disappear.

Artificial Intelligence is reshaping truth. Blockchain is redefining ownership. Virtual learning is decentralising education. Global migration is rewriting identity.

In this high-speed reordering of the world, silence is not just dangerous, it is disqualifying. Africa cannot afford to be reactive. We cannot wait for permission from international publishers, validation from foreign academics, or rescue from distant donors. History has shown us that those who do not record their contributions are often written out of the narrative.

The time to publish is not tomorrow. It is now.

We stand at a crossroads. One road leads to further erasure, where our wisdom, languages, inventions, and spirit are left in the shadows. The other leads to authorship and agency, where textbooks teach our version of history, archives preserve our victories, and platforms allow future generations to say: We were never voiceless. We were just unpublished.

This is no longer a creative luxury. This is a civilizational imperative. Because the future will not ask who you were. It will ask what you documented.

"If we do not tell our stories, others will. And when they do, they will not tell them in our favour."

— African Proverb

Africa Will Not Perish in Silence

We are not powerless. We are powerful but unpublished. We are not voiceless. We are voices waiting to be amplified.

This is our moment to rise pen in hand, camera in focus, microphone on, archives open, languages honoured, elders recorded, truth unfiltered.

We must publish before we perish. We must document so we can define. We must write so we can rise.

CHAPTER FIVE

DOCUMENTATION IS WEALTH

Every great economic power in the modern world, whether the United States, China, Japan, or Germany, has built its wealth not only on factories and farmland, but on something far more intangible: intellectual property. Patents, copyrights, trademarks, blueprints, formulas, and media rights are now among the most lucrative assets on Earth.

Software code, brand identities, pharmaceutical patents, and blockbuster films are protected and monetised in ways that allow creators and corporations to generate wealth across borders and generations.

Africa, by contrast, remains rich in creativity but poor in protection. The continent holds an unmatched diversity of languages, music, dance, dress, design, stories, proverbs, oral histories, sacred rituals, traditional medicine, agricultural techniques, and spiritual knowledge. This vast reservoir of intellectual capital is both culturally rich and economically potent. Yet very little of it is formally recorded, legally protected, or strategically monetised.

When we fail to document what we create, we leave it vulnerable to appropriation and erasure. Traditional herbs and healing techniques are studied by researchers abroad and patented under foreign names. African fashion designs appear on global runways, sold at premium prices by companies that give no credit to the cultures that inspired them.

Songs originating from villages in Mali, Congo, or Uganda or Nigeria are sampled, remixed, and streamed worldwide, yet the original composers remain unknown and uncompensated. Even sacred stories passed down for centuries are adapted into bestselling books, animations, and films produced not in Africa, but in Hollywood, London, or Seoul.

The tragedy is both economic and existential. When someone else owns your story, they control how it is told, who gets access, and who gets paid. And when your stories are not recorded at all, you risk being erased altogether.

Documentation is the first step toward ownership. If an idea is not written down, it cannot be registered. If it is not registered, it cannot be defended. If it cannot be defended, it cannot be owned. And if it cannot be owned, it will not generate wealth for the communities that birthed it.

For too long, Africa has relied on memory instead of manuscripts, performance instead of publishing, and inheritance instead of intellectual protection. But in a world where data is currency and ideas are capital, we cannot afford to treat our cultural knowledge as disposable or secondary. What we document today becomes the asset base for tomorrow's creative economy.

True empowerment requires not only preserving our wisdom but positioning it as a competitive advantage. This means training our youth not only to create but also to copyright. It means encouraging artists, herbalists, designers, and storytellers to see their work not just as an expression, but as a business. It means building institutions that can support the registration, licensing, and export of African intellectual property on fair and equal terms.

Until we shift this mindset, others will continue to profit from our brilliance while we remain spectators to our own wealth.

Documentation is not a Western obsession; it is a universal strategy. It is how we move from being merely creative to being compensated. It is how we preserve our truth, protect our inheritance, and unlock prosperity not just for the few, but for the many.

Africa is not lacking in wealth. It is simply leaking through the cracks of undocumented genius.

Stories Sell. Culture Pays.

There is no doubt that African culture has a profound impact on the world. From the rhythm of Afrobeats topping global music charts to the visual spectacle of Marvel's *Black Panther* breaking box-office records to the enduring fascination with Maasai warriors, the Ethiopian highlands, and the Egyptian pyramids, Africa's stories already hold immense global value.

However, here's the dilemma: while the world eagerly consumes African culture, Africa itself is not the one profiting from it. In every major cultural industry, Africa is present but underrepresented, underpaid, and under-published. Consider the numbers:

The global **book publishing industry** is worth over **$150 billion annually**, projected to reach **$192 billion by 2030**. The **music streaming industry** generates more than **$47 billion a year**, expected to grow to **$108 billion by 2030**. **Film and television** bring in over **$270 billion annually**. **E-learning, digital education, and knowledge platforms** are projected to exceed **$400 billion globally**, with forecasts extending to well over **$2 trillion by 2035**.

These industries thrive on stories, identity, knowledge, and above all, content. And what is content, if not documentation?

Yet Africa's share of these booming sectors remains minuscule. The continent is often the subject, but rarely the publisher. Our creatives produce brilliance yet face obstacles at every step: lack of access to capital, limited publishing infrastructure, absence of legal protection, and policies that stifle rather than support creative entrepreneurship.

We see young artists with global appeal recording songs in improvised home studios, writers printing books one copy at a time, and filmmakers pleading for international distribution that rarely comes. This is not due to a lack of talent; Africa is rich in it. It is due to a lack of systems.

The current structure ensures that while Africa inspires content, others capitalise on it. Our stories fuel billion-dollar industries abroad while our creatives struggle to make a living.

Nonetheless, it doesn't have to stay this way.

What Africa needs is not more proof that its culture is valuable; we have already proven that. What we need is a publishing and content ecosystem that captures that value, retains it, and reinvests it locally. A system that transforms African storytelling into African economic power.

Every folktale, proverb, ritual, historical account, and contemporary narrative must be transformed into books, audio series, animated films, short-form documentaries, apps, lesson plans, and metaverse experiences. Authors, elders, historians, dancers, and designers deserve platforms to share their gifts not only with their immediate communities but with the global market. This is how Africa's wisdom becomes both timeless and borderless.

The audience is already there. The world is hungry for authentic, diverse, and rooted content.

To unlock this opportunity, we must act intentionally. We must establish publishing houses that prioritise African voices. We must digitise archives and fund translations of our literature into global languages. We must create royalty systems that protect and pay creatives fairly.

We must train the next generation not only to tell stories but to license and own them. We must fund creative hubs, studios, and accelerators that provide scalable infrastructure. And we must embrace new distribution channels from streaming platforms to blockchain royalties and AI-powered marketplaces.

Documentation is not just a cultural act. It is a business model. With the right investment and coordination, a thriving African documentation ecosystem could generate billions in local and international revenue. It would stimulate job creation across various sectors, including education, technology, publishing, tourism, fashion, music, and media. It would make our economies not just resource-rich but idea-rich.

Africa's future will not be built on extraction alone but on expression. And in the global economy, those who tell the stories control the value.

Documentation Creates Jobs

When most people think of documentation, they imagine dusty libraries or forgotten archives. In reality, documentation is a dynamic, living process, one that, if intentionally developed, can ignite job creation across dozens of industries.

Publishing is not just about putting ink on paper or pixels on a screen; it is about building a value chain that touches everything from education to entertainment, from history to innovation.

Every time a story is written, a job is created. Every podcast produced is a pay check. Every archive digitised is an opportunity. From the moment a writer begins drafting a manuscript to the moment a designer lays out a book, a narrator records an audiobook, a translator adapts it into multiple languages, and a marketer promotes it to the world, work is being done. Real work. Skilled work. Work that empowers communities and fuels local economies.

This is not abstract theory; it is a tangible, scalable reality.

An investment in publishing activates different sectors: writers, editors, proofreaders, illustrators, and photographers form the creative chain. Printers, typesetters, and binders sustain the production line. Podcasters, animators, videographers, coders, app developers, voice-over artists, narrators, and sound engineers operate within the digital media spectrum.

Cultural curators, museum staff, librarians, historians, archivists, data managers, and translators uphold preservation and knowledge. Event planners, publicists, and distributors build the marketing and outreach arm. IP lawyers, copyright consultants, and contract negotiators defend the work.

Now, imagine if this creative value chain were intentional, supported, and scaled.

Picture a continent where every region has a Cultural Documentation Hub, a vibrant space where young people are trained to capture oral traditions, preserve local dialects, and interview community elders.

These hubs could offer publishing services to local entrepreneurs and authors, transforming their lived experiences into marketable books. They could conduct training sessions in podcast production and storytelling, equipping young people with the tools to create content for streaming and syndication. They could serve as tourist information centres, offering curated experiences around a region's history, crafts, recipes, shrines, sites, and songs.

The stories that once vanished with each passing generation could become the foundation of creative businesses, educational tools, and cultural exports.

These ideas are not distant dreams. They are possible. They are profitable. And they are sustainable.

The digital age has dramatically lowered the cost of content production and distribution. A young person with a smartphone today has more publishing power than entire printing houses had just twenty years ago. What we lack is not talent or technology, but infrastructure, investment, and a mindset shift to treat documentation as both a civic duty and a business opportunity.

Africa's youth population is exploding. Unemployment is high. The demand for dignified work is urgent. At the same time, the world is craving authentic African perspectives. Documentation can bridge these two realities, creating income while preserving identity.

When we document, we do more than preserve the past. We create the future.

A future with jobs.

A future with meaning.

A future where Africa is not only heard but paid.

Publishing Builds Institutions that Outlive Individuals

Great nations are not sustained solely by the charisma of leaders or the wealth beneath their soil. They are sustained by institutions strong, resilient, memory-keeping institutions that outlive any one leader, political party, or generation.

Libraries, museums, archives, universities, and research centres are the skeletal framework of every enduring society. And at the core of each of these institutions lies one unshakable foundation: documentation.

Documentation gives institutions life, direction, and memory. It is what makes learning possible and leadership accountable. It is how policies are reviewed, histories are traced, data are compared, and knowledge is passed on.

In societies where documentation is consistent, progress can be measured over decades. Leaders can learn from predecessors' successes and mistakes. Policies evolve from proven strategies, not guesswork. Governance becomes less about personalities and more about sustainable systems.

In societies where documentation is weak or absent, every new leader starts from scratch. Every generation repeats the same mistakes. Every innovation risk is being forgotten before it can be improved upon.

A nation without a documentation culture is like a business without financial records. It may be busy, but it cannot track growth, defend decisions, or plan for the future.

In Africa, the fragility of many public institutions is not just a governance problem; it's a documentation problem. Colonial administrations kept meticulous archives of our resources, labour, and resistance. Yet post-independence governments often lacked the resources, vision, or political will to continue that recordkeeping for the benefit of their own people. The result? Ministries, universities, and cultural bodies frequently operate with fragmented data and shallow institutional memory.

This lack of continuity is expensive. Education systems struggle to design curricula rooted in African worldviews because the knowledge base is under-recorded. Health ministries struggle to assess the long-term effectiveness of traditional medicine due to the scarcity of evidence, which is often anecdotal or scattered.

Local governments often fail to plan sustainable development because key information, such as land records, environmental data, or policy results, is incomplete. Conflict resolution efforts often falter because past treaties, tribal boundaries, and customary laws are undocumented or have been lost.

Now imagine a different Africa, one where documentation is embedded in every institution. Ministries could have digital archives accessible nationwide. Universities could publish African research in both academic journals and public repositories. Museums could partner with communities to record oral histories in local dialects.

Think tanks could draw on indigenous knowledge systems to inform the design of governance and development strategies. Libraries could function not as dusty relics of colonial textbooks, but as vibrant cultural repositories of the African imagination.

Such institutions would not rise and fall with election cycles or donor grants. They would endure. They would grow. They would serve generations yet unborn. Publishing is not just about books; it is about building memory. And memory is the backbone of identity, stability, and power.

Suppose Africa is to move beyond political independence toward true sovereignty of thought, strategy, and systems. In that case, publishing must be elevated from a niche pursuit of intellectual elites to a strategic national priority. Leaders will pass. Generations will pass. But what we publish can last.

From Content to Commerce: Pathways to Monetisation

Every story, every rhythm, every recipe, every proverb, every ritual is not just a cultural artefact. These are economic assets waiting to be activated. The challenge is not in creating them; we already have centuries' worth of creativity. The challenge is in moving from content to commerce.

The pathway is clear: capture, conversion, packaging, distribution, and monetisation. **Capture** is the first and most vital step: a grandmother explaining a birth ritual, a healer naming plants for wound treatment, a fisherman sharing tidal knowledge passed down for generations, a poet reciting verses at a wedding.

If these moments are not captured, written down, recorded as audio, or filmed, they vanish with time. Once captured, they become the raw material of value creation.

Conversion is the next stage. Captured content must be transformed into usable formats. A conversation becomes a book. A folktale becomes a children's animation. A memory becomes a podcast episode. A dance becomes a YouTube tutorial. A proverb becomes a graphic series for social media or even merchandise. The modern economy rewards multi-format content, something that can be read, watched, heard, or interacted with digitally.

Packaging is where creativity meets strategy. Packaging determines how a story is presented, to whom, and in what style. The way you present a folktale to schoolchildren is different from how you present it to diaspora academics or tourists. Design, language, and format matter.

A single Tanzanian folktale, for instance, could exist as a bilingual children's book for schools, a subtitled animation for YouTube, a podcast episode for heritage enthusiasts, or a short film for festivals.

Distribution is where many African creators face barriers, not because of a lack of talent, but because of a lack of access. Yet global platforms are now open to all: Amazon for books, Spotify and Apple Music for audio, YouTube and TikTok for video, Udemy and Teachable for courses.

Local distribution is equally important: community radio stations, local bookshops, cultural festivals, schools, universities, and even WhatsApp networks.

Finally comes ***monetisation***. Once distributed, content can generate income: direct sales of books, courses, or merchandise; subscription-based memberships; licensing for film, curriculum, or museum exhibitions; sponsorships from brands; crowdfunding for documentation projects.

Across Africa, creatives are already turning oral history into documentaries, tribal art into global fashion brands, and indigenous agriculture into paid e-learning platforms. What is missing is scale and system, making this process consistent and accessible to every community.

We must move from simply inspiring global industries to owning our share of them.

Tourism, Culture, and National Branding

Tourism is one of the most direct ways to turn culture into cash. But tourists don't cross oceans for a hotel room or a sunny beach alone; they travel for a story.

People want to walk where history happened. They want to savour food with a legacy, hear music that carries centuries in its rhythm, and witness rituals and architecture that embody their identity. In short, they come for the narrative. And narratives depend on documentation.

Every great tourist economy is built on published stories. Italy curates the Renaissance through books, museums, and tours. Japan turns centuries-old tea ceremonies into cultural experiences. Mexico markets Día de Muertos worldwide through literature, film, and art. These industries thrive because the stories were written down, recorded, and promoted.

Africa has no shortage of heritage worth travelling for: the ancient palaces of Buganda, the stone cities of Great Zimbabwe, the libraries of Timbuktu, the rock-hewn churches of Lalibela, the maritime history of Swahili city-states, the kingdoms of Benin, Mali, and Ashanti. But too many of these treasures remain undocumented or poorly documented, meaning they cannot be fully promoted, preserved, or monetised.

Reimagining African tourism involves creating curated storytelling tours, interactive museums with digital timelines, online exhibitions tailored for diaspora students, and multimedia archives that combine video, audio, and photography. These experiences would attract visitors, inspire investment, and create jobs in guiding, content creation, and heritage management.

Tourism without a story is just sightseeing. Tourism with a documented history is a form of nation branding.

When Ghana launched the Year of Return, it was not selling just a destination; it was selling a documented narrative of heritage, homecoming, and identity.

Morocco's medinas, Egypt's pyramids and South Africa's Robben Island all rely on published history to remain relevant and profitable.

Africa already has the culture. What we need is the strategy: document it thoroughly, package it for global audiences, and distribute it through tourism boards, online platforms, and cultural partnerships.

When we publish, we promote. When we promote, we attract. And when we attract, we earn.

Documentation as Investment, Not Expense

Across Africa, documentation is still seen by too many leaders and policymakers as a "cultural extra," something nice to have when budgets allow. Still, the first thing to be cut when money is tight. Roads, hospitals, and schools always seem more urgent. And while those are vital, treating documentation as optional is a costly mistake.

Documentation is not a decorative expense. It is infrastructure just as critical as power lines, clean water, and transport routes. When done right, it multiplies value across sectors. It strengthens identity, attracts investment, inspires innovation, and improves education and social cohesion.

Why is it a smart investment? Nations that prioritise documentation are better equipped to govern, innovate, and grow. They have memory and clarity.

A documented nation knows its history and can teach it. It tracks its progress and learns from past failures. It projects confidence to investors and partners. It builds policies rooted in reality, not guesswork.

This isn't sentimental, it's strategic.

Education improves when students learn from materials rooted in their own culture.

Tourism thrives when destinations have stories to tell.

Innovation accelerates when indigenous knowledge systems are recorded and adapted for modern use.

National pride grows when citizens see themselves reflected in archives, books, and media.

Documentation also signals stability to the outside world. Investors and donors are more likely to commit resources to a country that appears organised, forward-thinking, and rooted in identity.

Publishing your vision in policy papers, cultural catalogues, and national strategies is a way of saying, "We know who we are, where we've been, and where we're going."

Documentation is a development multiplier. Its impact stretches across governance, business, health, education, and diplomacy. In governance, it creates transparency and continuity. In business, it protects intellectual property.

In health, it preserves traditional medical knowledge and public health data. In education, it empowers teachers with culturally relevant curricula. In diplomacy, it strengthens a nation's negotiating position by controlling its own narrative.

Put simply, documentation pays for itself many times over. The challenge is to convince policymakers, businesses, and communities that it is not a luxury, but it is the foundation of sustainable progress.

Without it, we forget. We repeat mistakes. We vanish from the global conversation.

With it, we remember. We build. We compete.

Diaspora Dollars: Publishing Beyond Borders

Scattered across continents in bustling cities, quiet suburbs, classrooms, boardrooms, hospitals, and households, lives one of Africa's most underutilised resources: its diaspora.

Every year, Africans abroad send billions of dollars home in remittances. That money builds houses, pays school fees, starts businesses, and supports entire families.

But beyond the financial contribution lies something deeper: a longing for connection, a hunger for identity, a yearning for belonging. And that yearning cannot be fulfilled by money transfers alone.

It must be met with memory.

For many diaspora children born in London, Toronto, Atlanta, Paris, or Sydney, "Africa" is an image sometimes colourful and romantic, sometimes distorted by stereotypes, but often fragmented. They may know only bits and pieces of their heritage, learned through scattered conversations, brief holiday visits, or second-hand media portrayals.

The challenge? Their parents want to pass on their culture but often lack the materials to do so. There are too few children's books in African languages, too few documentaries that reflect African values, and too few educational tools that teach Africa's history from an African perspective.

This leads to identity erosion. Over time, language fluency fades, cultural pride weakens, and shallow impressions replace the deep roots of connection.

Publishing changes that.

When we document our histories, our philosophies, our customs, and our faiths, we equip the diaspora with tools for reconnection:

- ✧ A Ugandan mother in Birmingham can teach her children about Buganda kings using a bilingual picture book.
- ✧ A Nigerian father in Toronto can share Igbo proverbs through an interactive storytelling app.
- ✧ An African American teenager can explore the philosophies of Yoruba cosmology or Akan wisdom through podcasts and videos created by African scholars.
- ✧ A Jamaican tracing roots to Ghana can watch a documentary about the transatlantic slave trade told from our perspective.

This is more than just content; it is medicine. It heals disconnection, restores dignity, and builds bridges across oceans.

The diaspora is ready and eager. They are actively seeking authentic, high-quality African content: books in native languages, films with African storytellers at the helm, online courses in African entrepreneurship, agriculture, herbal medicine, art, and spirituality.

They are buying what we have not yet published.

Publishing Africa's story must be seen not only as a local project, but as a global mission. The diaspora is both a market and a movement. And movements need narratives.

When we publish, we give them language to describe themselves, context to understand their heritage, and confidence to pass it on. When we monetise our memory, we create wealth that flows both ways back home and abroad in cash, connection, and cultural pride.

Women, Youth, and the Creative Economy

If Africa is to unlock its economic and cultural potential, it must invest in women and youth not as recipients of charity, but as drivers of a creative revolution.

Across the continent, women hold vast archives of lived knowledge: songs, recipes, remedies, rituals, social wisdom, craft skills, oral histories, agricultural techniques, and family genealogies. Yet so much of this knowledge is undocumented, passed only through oral tradition and at constant risk of disappearing.

Imagine a rural healer in Senegal with decades of experience in childbirth techniques. Her methods could form the basis of a continent-wide maternal health guide. But if her knowledge is never recorded, it dies with her.

On the other hand, Africa's youth are overflowing with digital fluency, creative ambition, and cultural confidence. They speak the language of memes, apps, animations, music videos, and gaming. They remix tradition with innovation daily.

Documentation is the bridge between the wisdom of elders and the energy of youth. It transforms a grandmother's memory into a multimedia course, a tailor's dressmaking techniques into an e-learning program, and a village dance into a viral video series.

This exchange creates both cultural preservation and economic opportunity.

When women document, they gain voice and visibility. When youth document, they shape the culture to come. What's missing is the infrastructure, publishing tools, funding, mentorship, distribution platforms, and policies that protect creative rights.

An inclusive creative economy must bring in rural women, informal traders, teachers, artisans, and young content creators, not just elite artists or tech startups. Documentation democratises access and expands participation. Wealth is created when knowledge is transferred. And documentation is the vehicle.

The Cost of Delay

Every day we fail to document, we lose something that can never be regained.

A language vanishes when its last speaker passes away.

A ritual disappears when no one remembers the steps.

A story dies when its only storyteller remains silent.

A billion-dollar idea evaporates because it was never written down.

Delay is expensive. Silence is deadly.

Without documentation, our past fades, our present weakens, and our future is negotiated without us. Publishing must be treated as an urgent budgeted, planned, mobilised, and invested in at every level. Governments must integrate documentation into national development plans. Communities must create spaces for storytelling and preservation. Schools must teach not just reading and writing, but recording and archiving. NGOs and businesses must fund and scale documentation initiatives.

Documentation is not a soft issue. It is the foundation of progress, sovereignty, and survival.

Conclusion: Wealth Is the Story You Own

Wealth is more than money. It is the story you own. It is the name you protect. It is the wisdom you pass down. It is the legacy you leave. And all of it depends on documentation.

To publish is to build.
To write is to rise.
To archive is to advance.
To preserve is to empower.
Africa is not poor. Africa is unwritten.
Let us write ourselves into dignity.
Let us write ourselves into policy.
Let us write ourselves into history.
Let us write ourselves into power.
The future will not ask who you were, it will ask what you documented.

CHAPTER SIX

WHO SHOULD PUBLISH AFRICA?

"Every African is a storyteller. Every community is an archive. The question is not who can, but who will?"
— Geoffrey Semaganda.

The responsibility to publish Africa cannot rest on a few shoulders. This is not a task for ministries of culture alone. It is not the exclusive work of academics, novelists, or historians. This mission is too urgent, too vast, and too vital to be outsourced to specialists. To publish Africa is to preserve its identity, protect its legacy, and power its future, and that responsibility belongs to all of us.

From rural villages to bustling cities, from elders to students, from tech entrepreneurs to farmers, everyone has a role to play in building a continent that documents itself with confidence and care. Africa is not short on stories. It is short on publishers of memory on people who understand that to capture a moment, a song, a ritual, a proverb, or a testimony is to contribute to the continent's collective wealth.

Let us examine the distinct roles that various players must assume, beginning with the most crucial and often overlooked: the individual.

Individuals: The First Custodians of Memory.

Before there are institutions, publishers, or platforms, there are people. And every African, regardless of education, profession, or location, is a walking archive.

You are a custodian of memory.

Within you are stories of migration, survival, love, disappointment, success, faith, and transformation. Your family carries tales of weddings and funerals, harvests and hardships, home remedies and hidden traditions. Your own life is filled with lessons about what it means to be African in this age of change, movement, and reinvention.

If each person on the continent wrote just one story, Africa would overflow with books. And yet, too many voices remain silent not because they have nothing to say, but because they've been convinced that only "experts" can document history.

That lie must be dismantled.

You don't need to be a professional writer to get started. You do not need to speak in polished English or use academic jargon. What matters is honesty, clarity, and intention. The most powerful stories are often told by ordinary people who dared to speak truthfully.

Start where you are.

Write down the names and stories of your grandparents. Record your parents talking about their youth, courtship, work, and losses. Keep a journal of your own journey, what you've seen, what you've survived, what you believe.

Document the recipes you learned in your kitchen, the rituals you've observed, the dances you performed, the prayers you were taught. These are not small things. They are the raw material of legacy.

The digital age has made publishing more accessible than ever. With a smartphone and an internet connection, you can blog your reflections, film short interviews, or write a memoir. You can publish a recipe book on Amazon, share folk stories on YouTube, or launch a podcast from your bedroom. What used to require permission now only requires passion.

In doing so, you not only preserve your memory but also empower others. You give a voice to your lineage. You build a bridge for future generations to walk across, learning not just what happened, but how it felt. You turn your life into a map, your memory into a mirror, your voice into value.

This is where Publishing Africa truly begins, not in a ministry office or international newsroom, but in the quiet act of an individual choosing to remember, to record, and to release their truth to the world.

You are the first publisher of your people. And history is waiting for your manuscript.

Families: Protecting Lineage and Legacy

In African tradition, family is sacred. It is not merely the nuclear unit of parents and children; it is the wide, interwoven network of grandparents, aunties, uncles, cousins, clans, ancestors, and descendants. It is the place where identity is formed, values are passed down, and a sense of belonging is nurtured.

And yet, for all its depth and importance, most African families today have no written record of who they are, where they come from, or what they stand for.

This is a quiet tragedy.

As someone who has worked to trace my own family's journey, I've felt the pain of missing information, names we can't remember, land claims we can't prove, or stories that exist only as fragmented whispers. In my own lineage, we began the journey of documenting our heritage not out of vanity but out of necessity. We realised that memory, when undocumented, dies too quickly. And when memory dies, so does the inheritance of identity.

For much of my life, I was unaware of my lineage. I could only recall the name of one grandfather. Beyond that, everything was a blur. I could not name more than two or three generations. That ignorance left me disconnected, rootless in a sense.

But once I took the time to trace and document my genealogy, something changed. Today, I know the entire list of my ancestors stretching back through generations. I understand where I belong in my clan and how my story fits into a larger cultural fabric.

That knowledge filled me with pride. It made me feel more attached to my people, more responsible toward them, and more aware of how they could support me and how I could support them in return. I now see opportunities that we never shared before, simply because we didn't know one another fully.

When I was younger, no one taught me that my clan, my culture, and my lineage carried such deep value. I didn't know how my story connected to other tribes, or how intertwined we really are as Africans.

However, with that knowledge, I now feel more appreciative and accepting. I see that the differences between us are few compared to the vast common ground we share. That understanding gives me hope that, if we preserve and document our family stories, we can also preserve our collective African future. And it begins right where it always has, with family.

Too many families have lost property because land titles were never written or preserved. Too many children grow up disconnected from their ancestral clans because no one wrote down the migration stories. Too many values have faded because there was no record of the proverbs, prayers, or rituals that once held the family together.

Documentation is how we preserve the soul of the family across generations.

Imagine this: a family deciding to create a "House of Heritage," a physical or digital archive that contains not only a family tree, but photos from past generations, recorded testimonies from elders, scanned copies of land agreements, handwritten recipes, letters, voice notes, wedding footage, stories of migration, and reflections from each generation. This is more than nostalgia. It is an inheritance of knowledge. It is wealth across time.

Families must see themselves not just as caretakers of property, but as publishers of lineage. Writing down your family history is not something to be delayed until retirement. It is urgent work. It gives your children pride. It anchors them in a world that often tries to uproot them. It helps them walk taller, knowing where they come from and who they represent.

Moreover, there is economic potential hidden in family documentation. A family that records its entrepreneurial journey can publish it as a guidebook for future generations.

A grandmother's wisdom about medicinal plants can become a family-owned health manual. A family recipe book can become a source of income. A shared story of resilience through war or exile can be adapted into a screenplay, podcast, or educational curriculum.

Documentation transforms family memory into intellectual property, and that can be licensed, published, monetised, and celebrated.

More importantly, it becomes part of the continent's collective archive. Because every African family is a thread in the wider tapestry of Africa's story. When families publish, they don't just protect themselves; they protect a piece of Africa.

Start small. Write names. Record stories. Scan documents. Ask questions. Gather photos. Preserve what you can, while you can. Do it not just for yourself, but for the unborn children who will one day ask, *"Who are we?"*

Let your family have an answer not from legend, but from record.

Communities: Archives of Collective Wisdom in Africa

The community is more than a geographic location; it is a living library. A place where wisdom is shared not through textbooks but through fireside storytelling, song, ritual, proverb, and lived experience.

From the griots of West Africa to the herbalists of southern Africa, from the elders who name children at birth to the spiritual leaders who interpret dreams, our communities are filled with wisdom keepers, storytellers, and cultural curators.

Too much of this knowledge remains undocumented. It is passed from mouth to ear, generation to generation, vulnerable to loss with every passing elder. The death of a village elder should not mean the death of an entire worldview, but without documentation, that is exactly what happens.

African communities are treasure troves of oral tradition and indigenous knowledge. Every birth ceremony, initiation rite, marriage custom, and harvest ritual carries within it layers of meaning about identity, gender, morality, spirituality, and the relationship between humanity and nature. This is the kind of knowledge that cannot be imported. It cannot be Googled. It must be gathered, preserved, and passed on by us.

Communities must begin to see themselves as living archives, not just carriers of culture but publishers of it. This work need not be complicated. It begins with intentionality.

Appointing local "memory keepers," trusted elders, teachers, youth leaders, or pastors can serve as a starting point. Their role? To gather and record stories from across the village or neighbourhood. These could be oral interviews with elders, recordings of traditional songs, written accounts of communal rituals, or even photo documentation of cultural events. These guardians of memory can help ensure that the richness of community life is not buried with time.

Communities can host storytelling nights at local schools, churches, mosques, or community centres, intergenerational gatherings where elders share tales, children perform skits, and songs and proverbs are exchanged in celebration of local history.

Let's take it further. Let's ensure every festival performance is recorded, archived, and later transformed into a local history book or documentary. What begins as a celebration must become preservation.

In partnership with schools, youth groups, or even local government, communities can initiate grassroots history projects mapping village ancestry, recording traditional land boundaries, collecting folk tales in local dialects, and compiling village songs or proverbs into printed or digital collections. Such projects can be woven into community development efforts, part of the same strategic planning that goes into building clinics, schools, or clean water systems.

Because documentation is infrastructure, too. Cultural infrastructure.

It roots people in their past and prepares them for the future. It affirms belonging. It strengthens identity. It allows development to be contextual, rather than being copied and pasted from outside. When people know their roots, they walk taller, work harder, and dream bigger. They see that they are not just recipients of aid or subjects of statistics, they are heirs to greatness, authors of their own destiny.

Communities must rise to preserve their collective memory, not just for museums or tourists, but for themselves, their children, and their grandchildren. Every village has a story. Every neighbourhood has a hero. Every community has a legacy worth recording.

Let no community be forgotten because no one bothered to write it down.

Youth: The Digital Scribes of the New Africa.

Africa is a young continent. With over 60% of its population under the age of twenty-five, youth are not just the future; they are the now. And unlike any generation before them, they are growing up with digital tools in their hands, global culture at their fingertips, and the power to tell their stories in real time.

From Nairobi to Accra, Kampala to Kigali, Johannesburg to Dakar, African youth are already creating every day. They are making short films on their smartphones. They are writing poems on Instagram. They are designing fashion lines from home. They are remixing old songs into viral TikToks. They are filming their grandparents cooking and uploading it to YouTube. They are scripting web series in Pidgin, Sheng, Swahili, Yoruba, Zulu, Luganda, and French.

They are the digital scribes of the new Africa. What they need now is direction, tools, and recognition.

Publishing is no longer locked behind the gates of elite institutions. The Internet has made it possible for a teenager in a rural town to reach the world with one compelling video or blog post. The challenge is not whether youth have the ability; it's whether we will empower them with the vision to see their content as documentation, their voice as a legacy, and their creativity as capital.

Youth must be at the forefront of Africa's publishing revolution. They must be equipped and encouraged to use their digital fluency for cultural preservation, not just entertainment.

School projects can be turned into local history documentaries. Journal entries can become coming-of-age memoirs. Animated skits can teach ancient proverbs or recreate liberation struggles. Podcasts can amplify stories from grandparents, neighbours, and teachers. Apps can bring oral traditions to life for diaspora kids and global learners.

There is no shortage of stories. What we need are platforms, mentorship, and funding pipelines that support youth in telling their stories. Every youth hub, school, church, mosque, or university should have a storytelling lab complete with cameras, microphones, internet access, and basic editing software.

Youth should be trained not only in content creation but also in digital publishing, copyright, archiving, and media ethics. They should be shown that publishing isn't just for textbooks or politicians, it's for them too.

And when we recognise their work, when a young girl sees her poem published online or a young boy sees his video get featured in a local museum, they begin to understand that their voice matters. That their perspective is valuable. That they are not passive consumers of culture. They are producers of legacy.

Africa's youth already carry the rhythm of the continent. Their slang becomes language. Their fashion becomes a global style. Their dance becomes an internet trend. Their tech startups are reshaping how we buy, learn, and connect.

So, let's give them the tools to document, not just perform. Let's turn content creators into cultural curators. Let's invest in their capacity to record history, reframe narratives, and reimagine the future because when we hand a young African a camera, a microphone, a laptop, or a mentor, we're not just giving them tools.

We're giving them the keys to preserve our past, publish our present, and produce our future in HD, in real time, and in their own words.

Women: Keepers of Culture, Custodians of Knowledge

Across Africa, women have always been the keepers of culture and custodians of knowledge. They are the first storytellers, the first teachers, the first healers. It is in the arms of mothers, aunties, grandmothers, midwives, and market women that languages are kept alive, values are shaped, proverbs are passed on, and rituals are performed.

From naming ceremonies to funerals, from food preparation to fertility rites, from lullabies to liberation movements, women are the quiet architects of identity. And yet, their voices remain dangerously under documented.

In many societies, the contributions of women are often seen as informal or domestic, valuable, yes, but not formally recognised. Their wisdom exists in whispers. Their work is known in memory but not in manuscripts. And their worldview, which often carries spiritual, relational, and ecological knowledge, is rarely prioritised in formal archives or publishing systems.

To continue ignoring the voices of women is to erase half of our history.

We must change that.

Empowering women to publish is not about charity or inclusion; it's about survival. When women are silenced, whole dimensions of culture vanish. When women speak, generations listen. The stories they hold, from childbirth to conflict, from resilience to recipes, are stories that explain not only how we lived, but how we thrived.

Imagine if midwives across Africa documented their birthing techniques in manuals.

Suppose herbalists published books on plant-based healing. If grandmothers recorded their songs and lullabies for future generations.

Suppose farmers wrote field guides on intergenerational agricultural practices. If domestic workers and caregivers shared their social observations, reflections, and poems in community newsletters or online journals.

These are not romantic ideas; they are economic and cultural imperatives.

Publishing must become accessible to the African woman, not just to the urban elite or university-trained, but to the rural matriarch, the market vendor, the seamstress, the singer.

This means simplifying the tools. Offering workshops in community centres. Providing grants or stipends for women-led publications. Translating content into local languages. Building digital and offline platforms where women's wisdom can be recorded, preserved, and shared with dignity and pride.

It also means honouring traditional knowledge with the same seriousness as formal education. A mother's wisdom about raising children without modern technology is as valuable as any academic theory. A grandmother's spiritual insight or survival story is just as worthy of publishing as a political memoir.

In documenting Africa, we must be intentional about gender, not for the sake of inclusion alone, but for the sake of completion. A documented Africa that excludes the voices of women is an incomplete and distorted picture.

We need women not only in stories but also in telling stories. Not only in archives, but also in creating archives. Not only as mothers of nations, but as authors of nations.

To empower a woman to publish is to empower a people to remember. Because when women write, we don't just hear their voices, we hear the heartbeat of Africa.

Faith Institutions: Recording the Moral Soul of Africa

In Africa, faith is not peripheral. It is central. It shapes how people think, how families are formed, how communities are organised, how leaders emerge, and how nations persevere through pain and possibility.

Whether in churches, mosques, temples, or traditional shrines, spiritual institutions are often the most trusted voices in African society. They offer comfort in crisis, guidance in uncertainty, and meaning in a world that moves too fast.

And yet, for all their influence, many of these institutions have little to no written record of their journey.

Some churches have existed for fifty years but have no documented history. Mosques have generations of spiritual leadership but no biography of their imams. Temples have sacred teachings and prophecies that have never been written down. Traditional spiritual centres, where ancestral knowledge is passed through performance, do not have this wisdom down in print.

This silence is dangerous not because the faith is weak, but because memory is fragile. When spiritual stories and teachings are undocumented, they become vulnerable to distortion, misinterpretation, or complete erasure. In a fast-moving digital world, oral memory alone is no longer enough. If the moral soul of Africa is to remain alive, it must be recorded.

Faith institutions must rise to the responsibility of publishing not only to preserve their past but to prepare for their future. Religious leaders must see themselves as authors of the moral and spiritual narrative of their time.

Sermons, teachings, testimonies, dreams, visions, and community programs should be captured not only to inspire, but to instruct. What God did in one generation should be known by the next.

Let's ensure every church preserves its founding story, the prayers that led to its birth, the miracles that sustained it, the testimonies of transformation that defined it.

Let's turn Friday khutbahs into audio libraries.

Let's transform Sunday school teachings into children's books.

Let's help choirs record their original compositions.

Let's turn prayer points into devotionals and theology into curriculum.

These are not just religious resources; they are cultural assets, treasures of memory, and legacies of faith that must be documented and shared.

Faith institutions must also recognise their unique power to shape identity. For millions of Africans, the messages heard in worship services are more influential than those heard in classrooms or media. These messages must be grounded in truth, clarity, and context and made accessible through books, podcasts, pamphlets, and platforms that extend beyond the pulpit.

This work also means documenting the role that faith communities have played in nation-building. Churches, mosques, and temples have been at the forefront of peacebuilding, education, healthcare, and political transformation. These stories must be told not as institutional propaganda, but as part of Africa's collective history.

And it is not just formal religions. Traditional spirituality, often marginalised or demonised, is filled with cosmologies, ethical systems, ecological wisdom, and communal practices that deserve proper documentation. Rites of passage, systems of justice, symbolic art, sacred chants, these must be preserved with respect and scholarship, not reduced to myth or dismissed as superstition.

If faith institutions do not document their message, they risk losing it. The next generation may forget it or, worse, remember it wrongly. In an age of information overload, silence is not humility; it is surrender.

> The church must write.
> The mosque must archive.
> The shrine must record.
> The temple must teach beyond its walls.
> To publish is to protect.
> To document is to disciple others.

And to record is to redeem the truth from time's erosion.

Because faith is not just a feeling.

It is a story. And stories must be written.

Schools and Universities: Anchoring Truth in Education.

Education is more than just a system of exams and certificates. It is the process through which societies pass on their worldview, values, history, and dreams. What students are taught, what they read, what they write, and what they research shapes how they see themselves and how they see the world.

And for far too long, African education has been taught through borrowed mirrors. In classrooms across the continent, children still study foreign kings before their own heroes. They memorise European explorers but know little about African civilisations that thrived centuries earlier. Textbooks are often written in colonial languages, using imported frameworks, referencing Eurocentric thinkers, and sidelining African voices.

This is not just a content issue; it's an identity crisis.

To build a confident, creative, and sovereign Africa, we must rewrite what we teach. And that starts with publishing Africa not just as a subject of study, but as the source of knowledge.

Schools and universities must lead this shift. Every African university should be more than a place of instruction; it should be a publishing hub. Our campuses must become the engines of indigenous research, the homes of African intellectual production, and the custodians of truth told from within.

This means funding research that centres African contexts studies on local governance systems, indigenous health practices, ecological knowledge, oral literature, and cultural conflict resolution. It means encouraging student' theses and dissertations that explore their own communities, languages, and lived experiences, not just Western theories. And it means turning those projects into books, journals, podcasts, and digital content that circulate within and beyond the continent.

Let's raise a generation of students who write textbooks, not just read them. Let's fill school libraries with materials written by local authors and published in local languages. Let's establish academic journals in rural universities that publish research on the economic logic of traditional markets and the social structures of matriarchal clans.

Let's build digital archives where students can access stories, rituals, maps, and migrations specific to their people and place. This is how education becomes not just learning, but ownership.

This is not idealism; it is overdue innovation.

Educational institutions must also prioritise digital publishing. A continent where young people are born with smartphones in hand cannot be taught solely from textbooks printed in 1992. Africa must invest in open-access repositories, online libraries, culturally relevant e-learning platforms, and curricula that evolve over time and with technological advancements.

If our students can stream foreign music and comedy, they should also be able to access African history, philosophy, science, and literature from their devices.

This shift will require more than policy. It will require courage. African academics must challenge outdated systems and push for the decolonisation of curricula not just as a slogan, but as a practice. Ministries of Education must budget for African content. Donors and development agencies must fund local publishing, not just imported programs. And teachers must be trained to embrace local knowledge as legitimate, valuable, and teachable.

Because, when students read stories that sound like their lives, study solutions that come from their environment, and see scholars who look like them, their confidence rises. Their curiosity expands. Their identity deepens. And they stop seeing African knowledge as second-class.

They begin to understand that Africa is not just a case study.

It is a source of wisdom. A continent of thinkers. A classroom for the world.

Governments: Legislating and funding the National Memory

Nations are not built solely on infrastructure. Roads, power plants, and high-rise buildings may symbolise progress, but true development includes the preservation of memory. A country that does not know its story cannot shape its future.

And while individuals, families, and institutions all have a role to play in preserving heritage, it is governments that hold the key to ensuring this preservation is strategic, sustained, and secured for generations.

Without national leadership, documentation efforts remain scattered, heroic but fragile, passionate but underfunded. A grandmother recording lullabies, a teacher archiving local folktales, or a university compiling oral histories can only go so far. Without state coordination and support, these individual efforts risk disappearing like the very stories they aim to save.

Governments must rise to the moment. Documentation must no longer be seen as a luxury; it is a pillar of national development. It must be funded, legislated, monitored, and integrated into every sector of society.

National publishing boards should be established with clear mandates: to support local authors, oversee the production of culturally relevant textbooks, promote multilingual content, and manage translation projects that make African knowledge accessible across regions and languages. These boards can also partner with private publishers to streamline content that reflects national values and aspirations.

Governments must build and sustain national archives, but not as dusty, forgotten basements. These need to be living repositories of public memory. National libraries, digitised collections, and cultural centres should be accessible to all citizens, especially youth. These institutions should preserve everything from precolonial manuscripts and independence speeches to traditional music and community stories.

Legal frameworks are also essential. Too much of Africa's knowledge has been stolen, repackaged, and sold back to the continent by foreign corporations and institutions.

Governments must pass and enforce legislation that protects indigenous intellectual property, be it a sacred plant, a ceremonial design, or a native algorithm. Copyright laws, trademark protections, and patent support must extend to traditional knowledge holders and rural innovators, not just commercial entities.

Equally important is the integration of documentation into everyday life. Let's make it standard for every government hospital to record birth traditions and maternal health insights. Let's ensure every public school contributes to a local history repository.

Let's direct funds to cultural sites so they can preserve their rituals and oral traditions. And let's call on governments to launch nationwide documentation campaigns, practical, patriotic efforts that invite citizens to record their realities and share their heritage.

The creative economy also needs public investment. Music, literature, film, animation, and other storytelling industries must be supported through grants, tax incentives, and state-led funding schemes. Creative practitioners should have access to publishing training, digital infrastructure, and international markets with the backing of their own governments.

All of this is not optional. It is urgent.

Governments that fail to invest in memory are, by default, investing in forgetfulness. And **forgetfulness, on a national scale, is a form of cultural suicide.**

Without memory, societies fracture. Identity fades. Lessons are lost. Nations become dependent on imported narratives and foreign data to define themselves. But governments that choose to remember boldly, consistently, and strategically build more than monuments.

They build legacies.

Documentation should not be relegated to the corner of the Ministry of Culture's annual report. It must be at the heart of national planning embedded in education policy, digitisation agendas, intellectual property law, youth employment programs, and innovation strategies.

To govern is not just to manage the present. It is to preserve the past. And it is to prepare the nation for a future built on knowledge, not just cement.

Publishers and Media Houses: Amplifying the African Voice

In every society, the power to publish is the power to shape perception. For centuries, those who controlled the printing presses, the airwaves, and the headlines controlled the narrative. And when it came to Africa, the narrative was too often distorted, written by outsiders, edited by colonial interests, and amplified by institutions that saw Africa only through the lens of crisis and charity.

That time must end.

Africa must tell its own stories, and to do that, it needs publishers and media houses that are willing to amplify African voices, not just filter them.

From traditional publishing companies to digital media startups, there is a growing ecosystem of African-led platforms emerging across the continent. But much more is needed. Africa's stories are still too often inaccessible, underfunded, or spoken in languages that many Africans cannot understand. This is not just an issue of output; it's a crisis of access, diversity, and equity.

The publishing industry must evolve.

It must make publishing accessible to rural storytellers, indigenous communities, and underrepresented voices, not just elite authors from capital cities. We need systems that welcome oral historians, refugee poets, village herbalists, student journalists, and street philosophers. Everyone has a story worth telling; the challenge is creating platforms that honour and elevate those stories with dignity and reach.

Innovation is critical. In a continent where many people do not regularly read printed books but nearly everyone owns a mobile phone, publishing must adapt to embrace audio, mobile, video, and interactive formats.

Audiobooks in Luganda. WhatsApp serial fiction in Hausa. Illustrated children's books in Zulu. Self-published memoirs by market women, formatted for low-bandwidth access. The possibilities are endless if publishers are willing to let go of outdated gatekeeping and invest in creativity that matches Africa's diversity.

Translation must also become a publishing priority. Africa's linguistic richness is one of its greatest cultural assets, but also one of its publishing challenges.

Stories told in Wolof must be translated into English and French. Texts written in Swahili must be adapted for Amharic and Shona speakers. Without translation, we become strangers to one another, divided not just by geography, but by language. Translation bridges those divides and expands the reach of African ideas across borders, tribes, and generations.

Local stories deserve global platforms. We need more publishers who can identify talent and help package it for international distribution without diluting its cultural essence. We need book fairs that promote African authors to the world. We need partnerships with streaming services, literary festivals, and global distributors who see the commercial and cultural value of African storytelling not just as exotic content, but as an essential contribution.

As for media houses, their role is just as urgent. For decades, African media have too often mirrored the narratives of Western outlets: war, famine, corruption, and disaster. These stories are real, but they are not the whole story.

Media must reject the lazy, dehumanising trope of "poverty porn," the constant portrayal of Africans as victims, helpless and voiceless. We are not waiting to be rescued. We are rebuilding, innovating, creating, and dreaming. The media must reflect that truth.

Media houses should be platforms of pride, not pity. They must prioritise investigative journalism rooted in

African interests, celebrate everyday heroes, cover community success stories, and host debates that elevate the intellectual depth of African societies. They must invest in young talent, support documentary filmmaking, and collaborate with schools and communities to create content that educates and inspires.

Publishers and media institutions carry great power but also great responsibility. They are not just channels of information. They are the mirrors through which a people see themselves. If they distort, we forget who we are. If they reflect clearly, we remember our greatness.

Africa needs more than stories. It needs systems that protect and promote its own stories loudly, boldly, and without apology.

Pan-African Bodies and Institutions

Uniting the continent through the stories of Africa's more than 54 countries is a tapestry of shared histories, spiritual bonds, ancestral migrations, liberation struggles, and cultural symphonies that stretch across rivers and borders. The colonial map may have divided the land, but it never divided the soul. And yet, too often, our narratives remain fragmented, trapped within national boundaries, separated by language, and isolated in policy.

Pan-African institutions, like the African Union (AU), ECOWAS, the East African Community (EAC), SADC, and others, were created to bring the continent together: to harmonise development, promote integration, and foster a shared identity. But to truly unite Africa, we must go beyond trade agreements and summits. We must unify the story of Africa.

Publishing is not merely a cultural act; it is a continental strategy.

And Pan-African bodies must lead in ensuring that our collective story is preserved, shared, and amplified across nations.

The African Union and its regional partners have the mandate and the machinery to build a new publishing ecosystem, one that reflects the true spirit of Pan-Africanism. They must invest in a continental digital archive: a vast, living repository of African cultures, leaders, languages, liberation movements, artistic expressions, and traditional knowledge systems. This archive should be accessible across borders, in multiple languages, and designed to grow with time, updated by schools, researchers, ministries, and everyday citizens.

We also need cross-border storytelling initiatives, Pan-African anthologies, co-authored history textbooks, regional podcast series, and film collaborations that showcase not just one country's experience, but our shared journey.

Imagine a documentary tracing the story of African resistance to colonisation from Algeria to Zimbabwe. Or a children's book series that introduces young readers to heroes from every corner of the continent. These kinds of projects do more than educate; they build emotional and intellectual solidarity.

Pan-African institutions must also provide grants and funding for transnational research and multilingual publishing. African scholars should be able to collaborate across universities and countries, producing work that isn't confined by colonial language boundaries or institutional silos. A researcher in Mozambique should be able to publish with a peer in Senegal and be read by a student in Ethiopia.

Just as important, these bodies must create platforms for knowledge exchange spaces where ministries of education, culture, and ICT from different countries are able to share best practices in documentation, publishing, curriculum development, and language preservation. There is no reason for each country to reinvent the wheel. If one nation has launched a successful local publishing initiative, that model should be translated, shared, and adapted continent-wide.

This work cannot be left to NGOs or academic elites alone. It must be integrated into the official development agenda of every regional bloc.

Publishing Africa is as critical to continental progress as the African Continental Free Trade Area (AfCFTA), as essential as infrastructure, and as strategic as peacebuilding, since publishing must not stop at borders. The African story is a mosaic of unity in diversity. A chronicle of shared struggle, shared resilience, and shared hope.

To publish Africa well, we must publish it together.

The African Diaspora: Reconnecting Through the Written Word

The African diaspora is vast, diverse, and powerful, scattered across continents and time zones. From London to Atlanta, Toronto to Paris, and Kingston to Amsterdam, millions of people of African descent are raising families, running businesses, building careers, and shaping the global imagination. They carry with them the memory of their ancestors and the desire to reconnect with the motherland, not just through occasional visits or symbolic gestures, but through real participation in Africa's rebirth.

Financially, the diaspora is already making significant contributions. Remittances from Africans abroad inject billions into the continent annually, supporting schools, homes, healthcare, and businesses. Yet there is another form of wealth that the diaspora holds, often untapped: *their stories*.

Stories of migration. Of loss and resilience. Of survival and success. Of identity struggles and spiritual awakenings. These stories serve as a form of documentation that not only preserves the diaspora's voice but also offers a bridge back to Africa, a bridge paved in truth, healing, and shared humanity.

Diaspora documentation is not a side note. It is a central part of publishing in Africa.

African-born individuals abroad must be encouraged and equipped to share their journeys. From memoirs of adjusting to life in the West to children's books that explain African heritage to second-generation kids to essays on race, identity, and home. These narratives are not just personal reflections. They are historical records, cultural reference points, and tools for collective healing.

Beyond writing their own stories, diaspora communities must also invest in infrastructure. Imagine if every African in the diaspora contributed to funding a small publishing hub in their home district. In this space, local authors could receive training, access equipment, digitise oral stories, and publish their work. These are legacy projects. They are investments not just in memory, but in meaning.

The diaspora can also play a powerful role in translation and mentorship. Many children born abroad no longer speak the language of their grandparents. Bilingual books, co-authored by African and diaspora writers, can bridge that gap.

Diaspora professionals who understand global publishing systems, editing, distribution, marketing, and copyright can mentor emerging African writers and creatives, helping them navigate platforms like Amazon, Spotify, Substack, or Apple Books.

This is more than a cultural exercise. It is a healing mission.

For many in the diaspora, some wounds come from disconnection, being raised with a vague sense of origin but little tangible cultural grounding. When stories are documented, when a child reads about their tribe, their homeland, their faith tradition, or their family's migration, they begin to find language for belonging. They are no longer guessing who they are. They begin to know.

Publishing offers the diaspora a way to do more than give money. It gives them a way to give voice. It turns generosity into legacy, longing into connection, memory into momentum.

In doing so, the global African community becomes more than just a remittance engine. It becomes a living archive, a constellation of storytellers adding their chapters to the African story from every corner of the world.

Because the African voice is not limited to geography. It is global.

And it must be documented across languages, across oceans, across generations.

Global Allies: Partners, Not Narrators

As Africa rises to reclaim its voice, international allies, whether NGOs, universities, development agencies, philanthropic foundations, or publishing networks, must recognise their role in this movement. Their involvement is welcome, but it must be rooted in respect. Africa does not need saviours; it needs partners.

For too long, the global storytelling landscape has been dominated by voices that speak *about* Africa, not *with* it. Outsiders have authored our pain, filmed our suffering, edited our joy, and framed our complexity in headlines that reduce rather than reveal. **This must change.**

Global allies must support Africa's publishing revolution without seeking to control the pen. They must learn to amplify, not overwrite.

Support should begin with funding, but not for externally-designed programs imposed from afar. Instead, resources should flow into African-led projects, such as publishing houses, community archives, translation initiatives, creative hubs, and digital infrastructure built by Africans for Africans.

These initiatives already exist and are growing. What they often lack is consistent, strategic investment.

Capacity building is another key area. International institutions can provide training in editing, design, intellectual property law, and digital publishing, but this must be done in partnership with local ownership and with a long-term vision. The goal is not dependency, but sustainability.

Equally important is the need to shift away from extractive research models. Too often, international researchers come to Africa to gather data, only to publish it abroad with little acknowledgement or return.

Ethical partnerships must prioritise co-authorship, revenue sharing, and community access to the final work. Intellectual property must be respected, protected, and, in cases of exploitation, returned.

Africans are not voiceless. They have been unheard. Allies must come to the table not with pity or superiority, but with humility.

Support should never be about speaking for Africa; it should be about creating the conditions where Africa can speak, write, and publish for itself on its terms, in its languages, with its power.

Conclusion: Everyone Has a Role

Publishing Africa is not the work of one hero. It is not a job for one ministry, one generation, or one institution.

It is a **collective mission**. A **continental calling**. A **choir of voices rising together**.

From the village to the capital city, from the elder to the child, from the diaspora to the homeland, we all have a part to play.

The teacher is writing a textbook in Kiswahili.

The grandmother is telling stories on the phone to her grandchildren abroad.

The youth making TikToks that remix proverbs into poetry.

The midwife documenting traditional birthing practices.

The student translating folktales for school readers.

The community leader is organising a storytelling night under a mango tree.

Each one is Publishing Africa.

And together, we are writing a future where Africa is no longer misunderstood, misrepresented, or missing from the global story but present, powerful, and published.

> *"When the lion tells the story, the hunter is no longer the hero."*
> — African Proverb

Let us stop waiting for others to write our story.

Let us stop asking for permission to exist on the page.

The time to publish is **now**.

Not for profit alone.
Not for nostalgia alone.
But for **power, for memory, and for legacy**.
Because **when Africa writes, Africa rises**.

CHAPTER SEVEN

PUBLISHING BEYOND BOOKS

"Publishing is not just about books. It's about getting your message to the world by any means necessary."
— Geoffrey Semaganda

For far too long, the word publishing has been confined to a single image: a printed book sitting on a shelf. In Africa, this narrow definition has quietly silenced millions of voices and prevented countless stories from ever leaving the borders of their communities. It has created an unspoken assumption that only those with formal education, literacy in a colonial language, or access to a printing press can be "published."

But publishing is not about paper; it is about presence. It is the intentional act of preserving and sharing knowledge, art, and experience in ways that others can access, learn from, and pass on.

In the twenty-first century, this means far more than ink and pages. It means capturing a dance on video, producing a podcast in an indigenous language, creating an animation of a folktale, documenting a healing practice through photography, or livestreaming a cultural ceremony.

The digital revolution has blown the gates wide open. Today, anyone with a smartphone can become a publisher. A farmer in rural Tanzania can post a YouTube video demonstrating how to prepare a traditional soil treatment. A poet in Nairobi can upload a spoken word performance to Instagram. A teacher in Dakar can host a WhatsApp audio class on African history.

This is not merely a technological shift; it is a cultural liberation. The moment Africa embraces publishing beyond books, the continent will multiply its storytelling power, reclaim control over its narratives, and unlock entirely new economic opportunities.

Redefining Publishing in the African Context

In the Western tradition, publishing has often been equated with hardcovers, scholarly journals, and newspapers. These formats have their value, but they do not capture the full breadth of Africa's knowledge systems.

Long before colonial contact, Africans were publishing, just not in the ways that Western academia recognised. The griot in West Africa memorised centuries of dynastic history and recited it in public gatherings. The praise poet in Southern Africa delivered verses to honour leaders and mark historic events.

The elder in a Somali tea house recounted genealogies and clan histories over spiced tea. The drum circle in Central Africa used rhythmic codes to transmit messages across villages. The ceremonial dancer in Ethiopia conveyed stories through movement, embedding history and belief in every step.

These were and still are acts of publishing, because they preserved and shared information with an audience. Today, their equivalents take new forms.

A TikTok creator in Lagos translates Yoruba proverbs for young audiences. A rapper in Nairobi uses Sheng to critique politics and ignite debate. A Ghanaian podcast host explores African spirituality and entrepreneurship. A visual artist in Johannesburg uploads digital prints of Ndebele patterns to international design platforms.

The new African definition of publishing must embrace all of these forms. Once we broaden our understanding, we also broaden our opportunities for expression, preservation, and profit.

The Digital Renaissance: Africa's Time Is Now

For centuries, publishing in Africa was constrained by gatekeepers, colonial authorities, underfunded state presses, and foreign-owned media conglomerates that dictated what could be printed, in what language, and for which audience. Even when Africans created powerful works, their distribution was often controlled by outsiders, or their creations remained trapped within local communities.

That era is coming to an end, as, by 2026, smartphone adoption in Africa is projected to surpass seventy-five percent, while Internet access expands at unprecedented rates. Africa's population, the youngest in the world, is digital-first. They may not have easy access to a printing press. Still, they hold in their hands devices that can record high-quality video, capture audio, design graphics, and instantly distribute them to millions.

A mobile phone in 2025 is no longer just a telephone. It is a typewriter for blog posts, scripts, and social media threads. It is a film studio for documentaries, music videos, and short films. It is a recording studio for podcasts, audiobooks, and oral histories. It is a broadcast tower capable of streaming to global audiences in real time.

This is Africa's Digital Renaissance, a period during which the barriers between creators and consumers have been dismantled. The platforms are global, the tools are in our pockets, and the demand for authentic African content has never been greater.

We can already see the possibilities unfolding. YouTube channels feature village elders narrating precolonial history in their own languages, with subtitles for international audiences. Instagram Reels showcase traditional dances from across the continent, paired with explanations of their origins and meanings.

Podcasts in Swahili, Amharic, Zulu, and Arabic discuss climate resilience, spirituality, or entrepreneurship. WhatsApp newsletters deliver local news, health advice, and cultural stories directly to subscribers' phones. African authors now publish eBooks and audiobooks on platforms like Amazon, Kobo, Selar, and homegrown digital bookstores, reaching readers across the world instantly.

The key shift we need is from consumption to creation. Too much of Africa's Internet activity remains passive scrolling, watching, and reacting. True transformation will come when African creators consistently publish their own narratives, producing, monetising, and owning their content at scale. By doing so, they will not only reclaim Africa's rightful place in the global conversation but also build streams of income that bypass traditional economic barriers and empower communities.

The Power of Audio: Reclaiming Oral Tradition

Long before Africa had printing presses, microphones, or even written scripts in many regions, it had something far more enduring: the voice. Our ancestors understood that the human ear could carry the memory of a people.

Through songs, chants, proverbs, praise poetry, and storytelling circles, entire histories were passed from one generation to the next. Oral tradition was not fragile; it was resilient, capable of preserving centuries of knowledge without ever touching a page.

Today, audio publishing is not merely a modern media format. It is a return to our roots, an evolution of the very medium that once kept African history alive. What once travelled from ear to ear in village gatherings can now, through the tools of the twenty-first century, reach millions across borders.

Audio matters deeply for Africa because it breaks barriers that print and video cannot. It is accessible even to those who cannot read, making it invaluable in rural communities where literacy levels remain low.

It requires less bandwidth than video, which makes it easier and cheaper to share across Africa's mobile networks. It carries an emotional weight that text alone cannot match: the rise and fall of the human voice, the warmth of a storyteller's tone, the urgency in a poet's cadence.

And it holds unique potential for multilingual publishing. Producing content in multiple African languages is far more practical in audio form than in costly print, allowing cultural diversity to flourish.

The practical possibilities are endless. A Maasai elder could narrate life lessons in Maa, recording them on a simple smartphone and uploading them to a community podcast channel. A South African musician might create an audio series on the origins of drum rhythms, weaving stories with live demonstrations.

Health workers could deliver vital maternal health or disease-prevention messages as short voice notes in local dialects, sent via WhatsApp to remote villages. A youth collective in Ghana could gather oral histories of independence movements, edit them into a documentary, and share them on Spotify for the world to hear.

Audio is more than a tool of preservation; it is also a vehicle for commerce. Podcasts can carry sponsorships and advertising. Audiobooks can be sold directly to consumers or licensed to libraries. Local radio archives can be repackaged into educational materials.

Musicians can blend traditional instruments with spoken storytelling to create hybrid albums that function both as entertainment and heritage documentation.

It is worth remembering that community radio, the original podcast, remains one of the most trusted sources of information in African villages. Imagine if every community radio station recorded its broadcasts for archival purposes, produced audio learning packages for schools, or hosted regular "heritage hours" where elders shared stories and explained traditions. The impact would be immense.

By integrating audio-first strategies into Africa's publishing movement, we are not adopting a foreign tool; we are honouring and amplifying our strongest communication tradition. Audio enables us to preserve the voices of our ancestors while ensuring they resonate permanently in the digital age.

Video: The Universal Language

If audio is the heartbeat of African storytelling, then video is its face. It captures the gestures, colours, dances, architecture, facial expressions, and landscapes that words alone cannot fully convey.

In a continent as visually rich as Africa, video is not merely entertainment; it is documentation, education, and even diplomacy. A two-minute clip of a fisherman casting his nets at dawn on Lake Victoria can tell a thousand stories at once: stories of heritage, environment, skill, and community life.

Video is unmatched as a medium for Africa's publishing revolution. Its global reach is immediate. Platforms like YouTube, TikTok, Instagram, and Facebook Watch allow African stories to travel across continents in seconds. Its emotional impact is undeniable. Seeing the real faces, real places, and real voices of Africa challenges stereotypes more powerfully than a written argument alone.

Its versatility makes it indispensable: a single video can be used as training material, promotional content, documentary footage, or a school resource. And unlike fleeting oral memory, video has longevity once uploaded; it can be archived indefinitely, becoming a time capsule for future generations.

The practical applications are endless. Documentary films can explore heritage, migration, music, or traditional medicine, doubling as educational tools and tourism promotion. Miniseries can follow artisans, farmers, or innovators, showcasing real African entrepreneurship to global audiences.

Animated folktales can bring traditional stories to life for children, told in their own languages and distributed online or offline. Instructional videos can capture indigenous farming, weaving, cooking, or building techniques, preserving valuable skills while creating new income streams.

Behind every video lies an entire value chain. Creators, videographers, editors, animators, and scriptwriters form the core of the team. Distributors, broadcasters, online platforms, and film festivals extend their reach.

Monetizers, advertisers, sponsors, and subscription services ensure financial return.

Consider the potential: a traditional dance, filmed in a remote village, could be licensed as cultural footage for documentaries, sampled in global music videos, or monetised through YouTube ads.

A well-produced travel vlog highlighting African heritage sites could not only attract international tourists but also foster local pride and identity.

What once required expensive cameras and studios can now be achieved with a smartphone. Modern devices shoot in 4K, and free or affordable editing apps provide the tools to produce professional-grade content.

With basic training in storytelling, framing, and sound, even a teenager today has the capacity to create export-quality documentaries. There are no excuses; mobile filmmaking has made publishing in motion accessible to all.

At a continental level, the opportunities are even greater. A Pan-African Video Archive could collect and preserve cultural footage from every region, creating an invaluable record for future generations. **Governments could sponsor Visual Heritage Competitions in schools, rewarding short films that capture community traditions**. Tourism boards could fund influencer trips to heritage locations, ensuring authentic African representation circulates widely online.

The reason video must be central to Africa's publishing revolution is simple: images travel faster than facts. A single compelling video can undo decades of misrepresentation or cement a new, empowering narrative in the world's imagination.

In the digital age, if Africa is not seen, it is not remembered. And the surest way to be seen is to publish our stories in motion.

Visual Publishing: Art, Fashion, and Design

Africa is, in many ways, a gallery without walls. Everywhere you look, the continent speaks in colour, texture, and form: the intricate beadwork of the Maasai, the geometric murals of the Ndebele, the flowing drape of Ghanaian kente cloth, the symbolic scarification of West Africa, the vibrant street art of Dakar. Each is a language of its own, layered with meaning, telling stories of identity, belonging, and belief.

And yet, much of this visual language exists only in the moment. It is passed from artisan to apprentice, from mother to daughter, from tailor to trainee. Without deliberate documentation, centuries of creativity risk being diluted, appropriated, or erased.

Visual publishing matters because it places identity on display. A culture's art and fashion are not trivial ornaments; they are living archives of history, social values, and spiritual truths.

Visual publishing also matters because the stakes are economic. Fashion alone is a $2.5 trillion global industry, and African designers could own a far greater share if their work were properly documented, branded, and protected.

Just as important, visual documentation provides defence. By digitally archiving patterns, designs, and techniques, communities protect themselves from the theft and misappropriation that have long seen foreign companies profit from African creativity.

The strategies are clear. Traditional designs can be digitised textile patterns scanned, beadwork archived, pottery motifs preserved, and carvings stored in design libraries that schools, fashion houses, and researchers can access.

Photography books and digital galleries can showcase high-quality images of festivals, architecture, and attire, sold as coffee table collections, digital downloads, or even NFT art pieces.

Video archives can capture artisans at work, whether weaving, dyeing, painting, or crafting jewellery, with subtitles explaining each technique and its cultural meaning.

Fashion can be viewed as a form of storytelling. Shows that highlight heritage materials and designs, paired with interviews and lookbooks, can turn runways into living history lessons.

Education must also play a role. By integrating visual culture into school curricula and encouraging art students to document their communities, we ensure that the next generation becomes both custodian and creator.

The economic potential is enormous. Archived patterns can inspire international collaborations. Documented crafts can be sold through e-commerce platforms. Fashion brands can harness storytelling to command higher value in global markets.

Consider the case of a tailor in Accra specialising in a unique wax print. With visual documentation, her work could move from a market stall to the global runway. She could open an online store, feature in an e-magazine, and license her prints to fashion houses abroad. Without documentation, she remains invisible outside her neighbourhood.

And the story extends beyond clothing. Africa's buildings, from the mud-brick majesty of the Great Mosque of Djenné to the modern eco-homes of Namibia, tell stories of sustainability, ingenuity, and beauty.

Public art, too, from murals in Kinshasa to sculptures in Addis Ababa, represents culture in motion. Documenting these architectural and artistic expressions not only preserves heritage but also inspires innovation in future design.

The path forward requires deliberate action. **Each African nation should establish a National Visual Culture Archive.** Photographers and videographers must be trained not only in craft but in cultural documentation. Projects that digitise and distribute African art and fashion must be funded to ensure global reach.

Because when our images are preserved, our presence is felt. When our presence is felt, our value increases. And when our value increases, our people benefit socially, economically, and culturally.

Theatre, Spoken Word, and Performance

Africa's history has never been confined to parchment. It has been sung, danced, chanted, mimed, and enacted across generations. The continent's stages are not only theatres with velvet curtains; they are open fields, dusty courtyards, bustling marketplaces, and sacred spaces beneath baobab trees.

Performance has always been one of Africa's most powerful publishing platforms, carrying language, music, movement, and emotion in a single breath. It allows audiences not just to hear a story but to feel it, to embody it, to live inside it.

Performance publishing matters because it preserves living traditions. Dances, plays, and chants evolve with each generation, but when the key performers pass away, entire art forms risk disappearing unless they are documented. Performance also encodes community values, rituals often carry lessons about morality, leadership, history, and relationships.

And like music or film, performance is not only cultural it is economic. The performing arts can be monetised through tours, online streaming, cultural festivals, and training workshops, turning living traditions into livelihoods.

Africa's performance traditions are as varied as its landscapes. In Ghana, storytelling theatre blends music, dance, and proverb into a seamless performance. Along Kenya's coast, taarab music is performed in intimate spaces, mixing poetry with melody.

Nigeria's Yoruba travelling theatre troupes dramatise both folklore and contemporary issues, turning every village into a stage. South Africa's gumboot dance, born in the mines as a secret form of communication, is now celebrated as a global art form.

In Uganda, the Ndere Troupe weaves narrative, costume, and dance into powerful pan-African stories. Each of these is a living library, but only if recorded.

The strategies for publishing performance are practical and powerful. Live shows can be filmed with multiple cameras and high-quality audio, then stored in national archives and uploaded to platforms like YouTube and Vimeo for global reach.

Scripts and choreography can be transcribed into books or digital formats, with translations into African and global languages. Performances can be streamed, with virtual tickets sold to diaspora audiences eager to reconnect with their roots.

Anthologies of performance, as well as annual video or audio collections, could showcase the best of national or regional art forms, creating both cultural pride and revenue streams. Festivals, too, should have official documentation teams, ensuring that the energy of each event is preserved and packaged for education, tourism, and global distribution.

The economic potential is enormous. Performance tourism is already a billion-dollar global industry, with countries like Brazil and India leveraging festivals to boost their economies. Africa can do the same.

Documented performances can be licensed for international theatre festivals, adapted for school productions, or distributed to cultural institutions worldwide. Spoken word and storytelling events, in particular, hold appeal for brands and sponsors looking to align themselves with authentic African voices.

Consider the story of a spoken word poet in Nairobi. She performs to a modest audience of 200 people in a café. But her performance is recorded, uploaded to YouTube with subtitles, and suddenly it reaches tens of thousands. The video goes viral, and soon she is invited to international festivals, offered publishing deals, and allowed to release both a book and an audio album. What began as a small, local performance evolves into a global career, all because it was captured on film.

The steps forward are clear. African nations should establish National Performing Arts Archives that house video, audio, and script repositories.

Training programs for cultural documentarians specialising in live events should be funded to ensure quality preservation.

Partnerships with streaming platforms could create an "African Performing Arts" category, making it easy for audiences worldwide to discover and celebrate these traditions.

When African performance is recorded, it does more than entertain. It educates, heals, and connects. The rhythm of the drum, the rise of the voice, the sway of the body, these are libraries of movement and meaning. By publishing our performances, we ensure that Africa's soul does not fade after the applause.

Emerging Technologies: VR, AR, and Blockchain

The future of publishing is not simply digital; it is immersive, interactive, and intelligent. For Africa, this is not a distant horizon but an open door. The continent has an opportunity to leapfrog older limitations of publishing and embrace new tools that can preserve, protect, and present our stories in ways unimaginable just a decade ago.

Emerging technologies matter for African publishing because they multiply the power of storytelling. Immersion builds empathy: when someone virtually walks through a traditional village or attends a cultural ceremony in 360-degree video, they don't just hear the story; they live it.

Protection ensures ownership: blockchain technology can safeguard Africa's intellectual property, prove authorship and prevent theft. Interactivity engages the youth: Augmented Reality (AR) can transform a history lesson into an adventure, making heritage relevant to a generation raised on screens.

Virtual Reality (VR): Walking into Africa's Past and Future

VR headsets, once expensive luxuries, are becoming increasingly affordable. With them, African storytellers can build experiences where audiences step inside a narrative rather than watch it from the outside. Imagine a guided VR tour of Great Zimbabwe, complete with historical narration and animated reconstructions of the ancient city.

Picture an immersive kente-weaving workshop in Ghana, where viewers can stand virtually beside the weaver. Or a recreation of Nelson Mandela's prison cell on Robben Island, where visitors hear his voice echo his speeches as they look around the confined space that shaped a global freedom icon.

Augmented Reality (AR): Bringing History into Classrooms and Streets

If VR transports audiences to another world, AR brings new layers into our current one. Through smartphones or AR glasses, digital information is overlaid on the physical world, making history visible where it once stood. A student scanning a page in a schoolbook could see a 3D model of Timbuktu's libraries rise before their eyes.

In a museum, scanning an artefact could trigger a video of an elder explaining its significance. Tourists in Zanzibar could hold up their phones at the site of a ruined building and watch a reconstruction of the palace that once stood there.

AR empowers African publishing to transform every classroom, every street, and every public space into a dynamic textbook.

Blockchain: Protecting and Monetising Creativity

The blockchain, often associated with cryptocurrencies, is far more than finance. It is a decentralised ledger that allows for transparent proof of ownership and transaction history.

For African publishing, it could be a game-changer. Oral histories, songs, and designs can be timestamped and registered, making it far harder for outsiders to appropriate them.

Creators could receive royalty payments in real time when their content is streamed, sold, or used commercially.

Non-Fungible Tokens (NFTs) could secure ownership of unique cultural assets, such as a one-of-a-kind beadwork pattern, the master recording of a historic speech, or the digital replica of an ancestral mask.

The economic and cultural potential of these technologies is vast. Immersive VR and AR experiences can be sold to global audiences, generating heritage tourism revenue even when travellers cannot visit in person.

Diaspora communities could "visit" ancestral villages in VR or participate in digital storytelling festivals that bring them home across distance. Meanwhile, youth employment could expand as young Africans are trained in VR filming, AR design, and blockchain development skills that fuse technology and culture in industries of the future.

Of course, challenges remain. Access to equipment and training is uneven, but partnerships with universities, NGOs, and tech companies can close that gap. High production costs can be managed by starting with pilot projects and scaling gradually. Digital rights management is still evolving, but blockchain-based licensing can automate fair payments to creators.

The way forward is clear. A Pan-African Immersive Storytelling Lab could train creators in the production of VR and AR content. A blockchain cultural registry could safeguard African intellectual property. Partnerships with tech startups could produce AR applications for schools and tourism. An African Metaverse could be launched as a virtual environment showcasing heritage sites, festivals, and cultural experiences to a global audience.

Emerging technologies are not distractions from Africa's publishing mission; they are accelerators. They allow us to speak to the world in modern, memorable, and monetizable ways. When Africa's heritage is preserved in VR, made interactive with AR, and protected with blockchain, it not only survives but also thrives in the digital economy.

Multilingual Publishing for Multicultural Impact

Language is more than a means of communication. It is a vessel of memory, a carrier of worldview, and a guardian of identity. When a language disappears, a unique way of understanding the world disappears with it.

And when Africa's stories are told only in colonial or foreign tongues, much of their meaning, rhythm, and cultural depth is lost in translation. If publishing is to preserve and project Africa's true identity, then it must be rooted in African languages, not simply written about them.

Africa is home to more than 2,000 languages, each with its own idioms, proverbs, and cultural codes. A single proverb in Zulu, for instance, carries historical weight and nuanced meaning that may be lost when translated into English. Publishing in multiple languages safeguards authenticity, ensuring that stories remain grounded in their original context.

It also broadens access, allowing people who do not read English, French, or Portuguese to access knowledge in their own tongues. It strengthens intergenerational transmission, empowering elders to pass down wisdom in the language of their ancestors, rather than the language of colonisers. Most important, it builds identity: reading and speaking in one's own language fosters pride, belonging, and confidence.

The case for multilingual publishing is cultural, educational, and economic. It demands practical strategies that Africa is more than capable of developing. Translation itself must be elevated into an industry.

Networks of translators and interpreters trained not only in literal word-for-word rendering but in cultural context should be developed. Grants could encourage authors to make their work available in multiple African languages. Regional publishing hubs would strengthen this ecosystem: a Swahili Publishing Hub in Dar es Salaam, a Hausa Media Lab in Kano, or an Amharic Digital Press in Addis Ababa could ensure that content is created, distributed, and preserved where it is spoken.

Technology offers even greater possibilities. AI-powered transcription and subtitling tools trained on African languages can transcribe oral stories and automatically generate subtitles for video content. Schools can integrate local language publishing projects into their curricula, encouraging students to create magazines, blogs, or radio shows in their home language. Community workshops could invite elders to record proverbs, songs, and stories that are then digitised for local and global audiences alike.

Examples from across the continent show that this is possible. *The Bible translation movement has already proven that multilingual publishing can scale;* many African languages now have both written and audio versions of complex texts.

South Africa's literacy programs have produced children's books in all eleven official languages, boosting education outcomes and cultural pride. African film festivals increasingly subtitle their productions in multiple languages, making them accessible across borders.

The benefits are transformative. Publishing in multiple languages multiplies audiences: a book available in English, Yoruba, and French instantly spans three different markets.

The tourism and heritage industries also thrive when museum guides, mobile apps, and brochures are available in multiple languages, creating richer cultural experiences.

For the diaspora, multilingual publishing opens pathways of reconnection, enabling parents abroad to teach their children the language of their grandparents.

Challenges do exist. Translation is expensive, but this can be solved through crowdfunding, university partnerships, and AI-assisted tools edited by human experts. Skilled translators are in short supply, but publishing schools and cultural institutions can launch training programs to build capacity. Distribution barriers can be overcome through digital platforms that bypass the cost of print entirely.

The action points are clear. African Language Translation Funds should be established to subsidise multilingual projects. Content creators should be incentivised to produce at least one local language version of every major work.

Online repositories for African language eBooks, audiobooks, and podcasts must be created. And annual awards for excellence in multilingual publishing should recognise the pioneers who are leading this effort.

Language is not just words; it is heritage encoded in sound. Publishing in African languages ensures that the next generation receives not just what was said, but what was meant.

As Ngũgĩ wa Thiong'o once declared, "If you know all the languages of the world and you do not know your mother tongue, that is enslavement. But if you know your mother tongue and add all the other languages of the world, that is empowerment."

Publishing in African languages is not only good for culture. It is good for business, good for identity, and vital for the survival of our collective memory. When our stories are told in the voices of our mothers, fathers, and ancestors, they do more than inform; they transform.

Self-Publishing and Open Platforms

For centuries, African voices were silenced not because stories were absent, but because access was denied.

Others controlled the printing press, distribution networks, and capital. Traditional publishing, shaped by colonial systems and later dominated by Western corporations, acted as a gatekeeper, deciding whose stories were worth telling, in what language, and for which audience.

But the digital era has rewritten the rules. Today, the power to publish no longer rests in the hands of a few; it sits in the palms of millions. If you have a phone, an internet connection, and a story, you can publish.

Self-publishing means bypassing traditional publishers and taking direct control over the entire process from writing and editing to production, marketing, and distribution. For Africa, this shift is revolutionary. No more waiting for approval; creators themselves decide when and how to release their work. They keep full ownership of their rights and control how their content is adapted or monetised.

The financial upside is significant: self-published authors often retain up to 70 percent of sales revenue, compared to less than 10 percent in traditional publishing contracts. And the timeline is faster, a motivated writer can reach global markets in weeks, not years.

Today's online publishing platforms provide options for every medium. In books and eBooks, authors can use Amazon Kindle Direct Publishing for global reach, or homegrown platforms, which support mobile money payments and local currencies.

The Publishing Africa platform itself is emerging as a space built for African creators. For audio, podcasts can be distributed globally via Anchor.fm or Spotify, while Afripods caters specifically to African markets and languages.

Video creators turn to YouTube, TikTok, and Vimeo for global reach, or to Instagram Reels and Facebook Watch for short-form visual storytelling.

Writers of essays and thought leadership can publish on Medium, Substack, or WordPress, or contribute to community blogs and African-owned media platforms.

Across these ecosystems, the message is clear: every African voice has a place to be heard.

Why Self-Publishing Matters for Africa

The advantages are profound. Diverse representation and stories dismissed by traditional publishers as "too local" or "not commercial" can find their audience directly. Language freedom expands, allowing creators to publish in indigenous languages without asking for permission.

Digital distribution reaches the diaspora instantly, ensuring that African stories circulate both within and beyond the continent. And entry costs remain low, with most platforms free to join and additional expenses limited to optional services like editing or cover design.

Challenges and Solutions

Of course, challenges remain. Quality control is one: poorly edited or designed works can harm credibility. The solution is to build networks of affordable editors, designers, and proofreaders, and to establish peer review groups that raise standards collectively.

Another challenge is marketing. Many creators struggle to reach audiences, but workshops in self-publishing should include training in social media promotion, email marketing, and influencer outreach.

Monetisation can also be challenging, as many platforms tend to favour audiences in developed countries. This is where African-owned platforms and inclusive payment systems accepting mobile money, bank transfers, and local currencies become critical.

Finally, digital literacy remains a barrier. Not everyone knows how to format or upload content. To bridge that gap, Publishing Clinics could be set up in libraries, universities, and community centres to walk aspiring authors through the process step by step.

Self-Publishing as an Economic Engine

When self-publishing thrives, it fuels entire ecosystems. Jobs are created for editors, illustrators, audiobook narrators, and marketers. Businesses emerge from independent publishing houses to content agencies. New opportunities arise, including speaking engagements, licensing deals, merchandise, and online courses.

Picture a young woman in Kampala who self-publishes a children's book in Luganda. She sells printed copies locally, eBook versions globally, and licenses her illustrations for use in educational apps. One act of self-publishing becomes a chain of economic opportunities, built entirely on the power of initiative.

Building a Self-Publishing Movement

To make this potential real, Africa must treat self-publishing as more than an individual choice; it must become a movement. We need Publishing Ambassadors who guide creators from idea to launch.

Cooperative publishing groups can pool resources to share the costs of editing, design, and marketing. Annual African Self-Publishing Awards could highlight excellence and inspire others. Shared marketing platforms would allow creators to cross-promote, ensuring that audiences grow together rather than in isolation.

Final Thought

Self-publishing is not a second choice. It is a sovereign choice. It is how Africa can reclaim control of its narrative without waiting for permission from systems designed to exclude us.

In a world where gatekeepers are optional and audiences are global, the question is no longer, "Can I publish?" but "When will I publish?"

As I often say, "If you have a phone in your hand, you have a printing press, a broadcast tower, and a library. Use it."

Building a Publishing Ecosystem, Not Just a Bookstore

Too often, when conversations about publishing in Africa arise, the focus narrows to the production of books and their sale in physical shops. Bookstores, while important, represent only one link in a much larger value chain.

A thriving publishing sector is like a thriving agricultural sector: it is not only about the farm, but also about the irrigation, transport, markets, training, and preservation that keep it alive. In the same way, publishing must be understood as an ecosystem: a connected network of creators, platforms, infrastructure, skills, and audiences that sustain one another.

Why Africa Needs an Ecosystem Approach

Books alone cannot carry the weight of Africa's publishing future. Millions of Africans still engage with stories through oral traditions, audio, video, and social media more than through printed text. One-off projects, while inspiring, often fade quickly without structures of training, collaboration, and distribution to sustain them.

An ecosystem ensures not only cultural preservation but also economic and professional sustainability. It transforms publishing from an isolated art form into a viable career path and a thriving industry.

Core Elements of a Publishing Ecosystem

Creative hubs and coworking spaces are the beating heart of this model. In such spaces, writers, editors, designers, and digital creators can collaborate. They can host writing workshops, recording sessions for podcasts and audiobooks, or even operate small-scale printing and binding equipment. Mentorship programs can link established creators with newcomers, ensuring knowledge is passed on.

Government and donor support also play a pivotal role. Tax incentives for publishers, grants for local language translation, and public-private partnerships to digitise archives can unlock opportunities otherwise out of reach.

Alongside this, training and capacity building must become national priorities. Bootcamps under banners like "Publish Africa" could train schools, universities, and community groups in editing, design, marketing, and monetisation. Women, youth, and marginalised communities deserve targeted programs to ensure their voices are included.

Competitions, fellowships, and scholarships can energise the sector. Annual contests for short stories, poetry, documentaries, or podcasts provide visibility to talented individuals. Fellowships for investigative journalism or cultural preservation create depth, while scholarships enable young Africans to study publishing, creative writing, and media.

Infrastructure remains essential. Mobile recording vans could travel into rural areas. Regional labs could digitise manuscripts, audio, and video. Affordable printing services and eBook production facilities would make content creation possible at scale.

None of these matters can be addressed, however, without integrated distribution channels. Africa needs digital marketplaces, a kind of "African Amazon" for books, podcasts, and courses.

Partnerships with telecom providers could allow mobile money payments and direct content delivery. Integration with schools, churches, mosques, libraries, and cultural centres would ensure that published works reach the grassroots as well as the diaspora.

Publishing as a Development Strategy

In many African nations, publishing is still seen primarily as a cultural or educational activity. That mindset must evolve.

Publishing is a driver of development, shaping education quality, national branding, economic diversification, and social cohesion. A nation that publishes its own knowledge is better equipped to educate its children, defend its narratives, and inspire unity through shared stories.

Case Study Vision: The Publishing Africa City

Let's build a "Publishing Africa City" in every African region. Within its walls will stand audio and video studios, print houses, libraries, and public archives.

Tech labs will develop eBooks, apps, and VR storytelling tools. Training halls will host workshops and masterclasses. Marketplaces will showcase and sell African content locally and online. Such a city will not merely produce books; it will generate careers, revenue, and identity.

The Role of the Private Sector

Businesses can fuel this ecosystem by sponsoring content competitions, documenting their own histories, funding publishing hubs, and integrating African content into their marketing campaigns.

The Role of Communities

Communities, too, are vital. Local publishing committees could coordinate story collection, while "Documentation Days" could bring elders and youth together to record wisdom.

By supporting local authors attending launches, buying books, and sharing content, online communities breathe life into the publishing cycle.

Sustainability in the Ecosystem

For the ecosystem to thrive in the long term, revenue streams must be diversified. Sales, licensing, training fees, and sponsorships must all play a role in the overall strategy.

Creators must retain their rights and receive fair royalties. And a Pan-African Publishing Network must be established, linking countries in a web of shared learning, collaboration, and market access.

Too often, we imagine publishing only as the finished book sold in a bookstore. But the book is only the output. Behind it are dozens of inputs: writing, editing, designing, translating, recording, printing, digitising, marketing, distributing.

Each one is a skill, a career, and a contribution to the economy. And when publishing extends beyond books into podcasts, animations, video essays, virtual museums, fashion photography, performance art, and digital zines, the demand for talent increases even further.

Africa doesn't just need more authors. We need sound engineers, editors, narrators, designers, podcasters, videographers, translators, coders, curators, and digital publishers. We need **creative hubs** in every city and town, safe, equipped spaces where youth can record, experiment, collaborate, and learn. We need coworking studios with high-speed internet, libraries with self-publishing equipment, and mobile content labs to reach rural areas.

We also need policy and funding. Governments and donors must treat publishing not as a cultural side program but as a **development strategy**. That means:

- ➢ **Grants** for content creation.
- ➢ **Scholarships** for storytelling.
- ➢ **Fellowships** for filmmakers.
- ➢ **Incentives** for publishers who champion local voices.

Publishing must be written into national budgets, not as an afterthought, but as a pillar of education, culture, and the economy. Above all, we need a mindset shift.

Young Africans must learn that publishing is not just about books; it is about shaping identity, preserving memory, and creating wealth. It is not reserved for the elite. Their voices belong in the global conversation. They can write their future and distribute it.

Publishing must be seen not as a privilege, but as a power.

If Africa builds this ecosystem, the ripple effects will be profound. Jobs will emerge. Languages will be revived. Marginalised voices will find platforms. Local economies will grow through creativity and pride.

This is not fantasy. It is a strategy. We must not settle for selling books.

We must build the systems that birth authors, amplify voices, and transform communities.

Conclusion: Publish the Message, Not Just the Manuscript

"Don't just write the book. Film the dance. Record the voice. Code the memory. Paint the struggle. Animate the wisdom. Publish it all."

— Geoffrey Semaganda

Africa's story was never meant to be contained in pages alone.

It dances in our footsteps. It echoes in our drums. It weaves through our hair. It shimmers in our fabrics. And now, it flows through our apps and algorithms.

Our story is multisensory, multilingual, and multigenerational.

If we only publish books, we silence too many. But when we publish everything, the poem, the proverb, the painting, the prayer, the performance, the podcast, then we become unstoppable.

Publishing Africa means publishing the entire continent of Africa. Not just our history, but our humour. Not just our politics, but our parenting as well. Not just our textbooks, but our TikTok videos. It means turning every medium into a megaphone. It means telling the world:

"We are here. We are wise. We are worthy. And we will not be erased."

Africa does not merely need more books. It needs a publishing environment where creativity is nurtured, skills are developed, and stories are distributed widely across every possible format. A bookstore sells finished products. An ecosystem creates them, supports them, and ensures they endure.

I often say, "A bookstore is a window. An ecosystem is the whole house. Africa deserves the house."

Because the story of Africa is not yet finished, it unfolds one voice, one image, one post, one page at a time.

Let us publish it boldly.
Let us publish it now.
Let us publish it all.

CHAPTER EIGHT

THE ACTION WEALTH PUBLISHING MODEL

"Africa doesn't just need more writers. It needs publishing systems tested, accessible, and built by Africans for Africa."
— **Geoffrey Semaganda.**

After decades of helping entrepreneurs, thought leaders, and community builders publish their stories and knowledge across the globe, I've come to a simple truth:

Every African has a book in them. And every book has the power to change lives if the right system is in place.

The problem isn't a lack of talent. It's a lack of structure. We don't suffer from a shortage of wisdom or experience. We suffer from systems that don't know how to extract, refine, package, and distribute that wisdom in formats the world respects and pays for.

Publishing is not writing alone. It is access, infrastructure, mentorship, and monetisation. It's about giving people the tools and steps to go from, "I have something to say" to, "I've built something that will outlive me."

That's why I built the *Action Wealth Publishing Model,* a system rooted in African realities but designed for global impact. It's not just a publishing service. It's a pathway. A method. A mission. And now, it's time to open it up to the continent.

From Pain to Purpose: The Origin of the Model

I didn't set out to build a publishing company. I set out to tell my story, and in the process, I discovered how many others were struggling to do the same.

Growing up in Uganda, I lived through war. I remember seeing the bodies of those who had been killed lined up on the streets, and then one day they were gone, removed, as though their lives and their stories had never mattered.

In school, we were taught songs and cultural lessons that carried deep meaning, but because they were never documented, we were made to believe they were not important, not valuable. Speaking our local language was discouraged and dismissed as useless. Kiswahili, I was told, was for soldiers, for men who killed. The message was clear: everything that was ours carried a negative weight.

That silence, that erasure, shaped how we saw ourselves and still echoes today when young Africans grow up believing that who they are is not good enough.

Yet the truth is, rich oral traditions surrounded me. Elders who could recount lineages stretching back centuries. Proverbs that packed the wisdom of generations. Songs that held the memory of battles won, families built, and kingdoms formed. But almost none of it was written down. And the little that was often got buried, forgotten, or misrepresented.

Later, when I moved to the UK, I realised something that changed my life forever: what is written down is respected. Contracts were honoured. Books were cited. Policies were built on documentation. Identity, legality, and legitimacy were all founded not on emotion, but on evidence on paper.

It didn't take long to see the difference. Africa had the wisdom, but the West had the systems. We had the story, but they had the publishing power. That contrast began to burn within me a quiet fire that would define my path.

When I tried to find a job or make a living, I was told something simple yet profound: ***anything you want to do, someone has already done it, and they've written a book about it.*** There's always a workshop, a seminar, a manual, a mentor, or a teacher ready to show you how.

So, I began attending workshops and seminars, eager to learn. And soon, I saw a pattern. The people standing on those stages the ones commanding rooms, earning trust, and shaping industries were not always the most gifted. They were the most documented. They had written books. Their words gave them authority. Their documentation gave them power.

That realisation became my turning point. I was just teenager, in a new country, without family, without language or a name anyone knew. I understood that if I wanted to rise, I had to write. Those who wrote were seen as those who knew.

So, I began to write not for fame, but to survive. To promote my ideas. To find my voice. To make sense of my thoughts and share them with others. Writing became my bridge to credibility, my passport to possibility. I discovered a truth that shaped everything that followed: to grow, I had to teach; to teach, I had to document; and to document, I had to publish.

What started as a simple way to promote my business became a mission. I realised I could help others do the same to find their own voice, publish their knowledge, and turn experience into legacy. That was how my publishing journey began born out of necessity, refined through service, and built on the revelation that ***wealth itself is documentation.***

So, I began helping others publish not just authors, but entrepreneurs, pastors, coaches, teachers, and professionals each carrying a lifetime of wisdom but no clear way to share it. At first, it was small and personal. I hired experts to help friends outline their ideas, edit their drafts, design their covers, and navigate the unfamiliar world of Amazon. Soon, the demand grew. People were hungry not just to write, but to be heard. They wanted to own their stories to publish with dignity, with strategy, and with purpose.

That's when Action Wealth Publishing was born.

What started as a side project became a full model, a step-by-step publishing framework designed specifically for African and diaspora voices. A model rooted not in

Western templates, but in *our reality:* fragmented records, underfunded schools, oral histories, diaspora displacement, and digital disruption.

The model had to be flexible, empowering, and profit-driven, not just creative. It had to show people that publishing was not a luxury, but a ***tool for visibility, authority, and legacy.***

Over the years, this vision has grown beyond books. What began as a few manuscripts has multiplied into a movement. We've helped more than **750 individuals and organisations** across **over 65 countries** bring their stories to life publishing books, memoirs, guides, curricula, and manifestos. Along the way, we've also developed and documented **over 2,000 training and empowerment programs**, turning knowledge into action and ideas into institutions. From ministers to migrants, single mothers to start-up founders, educators to elders, and even refugees finding new beginnings each one carried a message the world needed to hear, and together, we helped them preserve it.

Some are published to *heal.* Some are published to *teach.* Some published to *market their business.* Others published to *start movements* or *build generational assets.*

All of them shared one thing: they needed a ***system***, not just a service. A partner who understood the complexity of African storytelling and the strategy of modern publishing.

That's what Action Wealth Publishing became: a bridge between message and market, between local wisdom and global platforms, between memory and legacy.

Now, we are opening that model to the continent and the world because publishing must not be for the few. It must be for *every African who has lived, learned, and longed to speak.*

The Core Framework: Educate → Extract → Execute → Empower

At the heart of the Action Wealth Publishing Model lies a simple but transformative four-stage process. It's more than a checklist, it's a journey of self-discovery, expression, and elevation. This model has helped people who thought they had nothing to say uncover stories that moved nations, and it has turned quiet voices into community leaders, founders, educators, and published authors.

This is the framework that enables both personal and profitable publishing.

Stage 1: Educate–Help People Understand the Value of Their Story

Many Africans carry life-changing wisdom, but they've been conditioned to think their stories don't matter, especially if they didn't go to university, speak English fluently, or write in perfect grammar. We begin by dispelling the myth that publishing is only for the elite.

We start with education not academic, but emotional and cultural. Through masterclasses, workshops, and one-on-one coaching, we help individuals reconnect with their voice and view their lived experiences as assets.

Whether they are mothers, farmers, healers, migrants, pastors, or business owners, we show them: *you are the expert of your journey.*

We also introduce them to the broader mission of the documentation crisis across Africa. People begin to see that their story isn't just personal, it's political, historical, and generational. When they realise that publishing their knowledge could preserve a culture, inspire a generation, or even shift a policy, something clicks.

They no longer ask, "Why me?"

They begin to ask, "Why not me?"

Stage 2: Extract–Pull Out the Message, Lessons, or Method from Their Life

Once someone understands the power of their story, we move to the next phase: extraction. This is where the gold lies, but it must be mined with care.

We use guided exercises, story-mapping tools, and structured interviews to extract the most valuable moments, messages, and methods from their life experiences. For those who don't write easily, we offer transcription services so that they can speak, and we help shape it into coherent content.

This process isn't just about information; it's about *clarity and connection.* We help them identify their book's central theme, the ideal reader, and the emotional journey the content should take them on. Whether it's a memoir, a manual, a manifesto, or a message, we help them get to the heart of what they want to say and *why it matters.*

For many, this phase is healing. It's the first time someone has helped them see their pain, passion, or profession as something publishable.

Stage 3: Execute–Package Their Story into a Product

Now, we turn the message into a manuscript. This is the most technical stage, but it's where dreams become tangible.

We guide each author through professional editing, ghost-writing (if needed), interior formatting, cover design, and ISBN assignment. Every detail is crafted to ensure their story doesn't just read well, it looks and feels excellent. We publish in multiple formats: print, eBook, audiobook, and even video courses or reels, depending on the nature of the story.

Then comes distribution. We publish through global platforms like Amazon, Apple Books, and Audible. But we also think local leveraging of regional bookstores, printers, cultural festivals, and online shops that serve African and diaspora audiences.

Our goal here is simple: to ensure their story is seen, heard, believed, ***and respected.***

Stage 4: Empower–Turn Their Published Content into Opportunity

Publishing is not the end, it's the beginning. A book is not just a finished product. It's a ***launchpad.*** Once a book is published, we empower our clients to turn their content

into an opportunity. Depending on their goals, we show them how to:
- ♦ Build a speaking career from their story
- ♦ Launch an online course based on their method
- ♦ Start a coaching or consulting program
- ♦ Use their book as a business card for partnerships or funding
- ♦ Create a legacy product for their children or community
- ♦ Raise money for a cause or build a following around a mission

We also connect them with branding experts, business coaches, publicists, and tech tools that can take their message to the next level. Because we believe that **knowledge should nourish families, stories should create a steady stream.** Publishing should create platforms.

This isn't just publishing for the sake of it. This is **publishing for a purpose. Publishing for positioning. Publishing for profit.**

This four-part framework Educate, Extract, Execute, and Empower has proven itself across cultures, sectors, and continents. It works for students, CEOs, single mothers, and government leaders. Because at its core, it honours the human need to be heard, the cultural need to preserve, and the economic opportunity to monetise wisdom.

And now, it's time to scale it to schools, villages, ministries, businesses, and beyond.

A Track Record of Results

The Action Wealth Publishing model isn't a theory. It's a tested and proven system. Over the past decade, we've helped transform lives, careers, and communities not by chasing trends, but by giving people the tools to honour their truth and turn it into something powerful.

Through this model:

- **Over 750 individuals** have successfully published books, manuals, memoirs, courses, and toolkits using our system.
- Our clients come from all walks of life from **first-time writers and single mothers** to **pastors, politicians, business leaders, and NGO founders.**
- Together, we've launched **more than 2,000 wealth-building products**, including online courses, coaching programs, workshops, speaking platforms, and digital resources.
- The reach is global, with clients across **over 65 countries worldwide**.

These aren't just clients. They are **creators of legacy**. They are **publishers of purpose**. And they prove, time and again, that when people are given the right structure, support, and belief, their message becomes unstoppable.

The system works because it was built for real people.
People with real struggles.
Real stories.
And a real ambition to make their life count.

This is not about perfection. It's about progress. It's about giving voice to the unheard, structure to the gifted, and dignity to the forgotten. That's the heart of Action Wealth Publishing, and that's the Africa we're building, one story at a time.

A Model for Publishing Africa at Scale

The Action Wealth Publishing Model was never meant to stay small. What began as a framework to help individuals extract and share their stories has evolved into a scalable blueprint for Africa's publishing revival.

If we are serious about preserving our identity, protecting our knowledge, and unlocking our intellectual wealth, then we must go beyond coaching a few clients or printing a few books. We must institutionalise the process, localise the infrastructure, and democratize access.

Here's how we can scale this model to serve *millions* across the continent and in the diaspora.

A. Training African Publishing Coaches

At the heart of this movement are passionate individuals embedded in their communities who can guide others through the journey of documentation and publishing.

The first step is to **certify regional publishing coaches** across Africa and the diaspora using the Action Wealth framework. These coaches would not only be trained in editing and formatting, but also in **story extraction, narrative healing, publishing strategy, and cultural sensitivity.**

Imagine a certified publishing mentor in every town, every university, every diaspora enclave **empowering others to tell their truth** and take ownership of their legacy.

These coaches would run bootcamps, school programs, storytelling clubs, and faith-based workshops. They would be the **guardians of Africa's untold stories**, trained not just to write but to raise voices.

B. Launching Community Publishing Hubs

To bring this vision to life, we need more than training; we need **physical spaces where publishing can happen**. Community Publishing Hubs would be the next frontier. These hubs could be housed in **libraries, schools, churches, mosques, community centres, or even tech incubators.**

Equipped with basic tools, laptops, internet access, microphones, cameras, and printers, they would become **safe spaces for creative expression, intergenerational dialogue, and cultural preservation.**

We would host regular Story Clinics, where elders are interviewed, youth are mentored, and families are helped to document their lineage. Each hub would become a **living archive of African thought, wisdom, and innovation.** With modest investment, a single hub could serve hundreds of people each year, producing books, videos, oral histories, podcasts, family trees, and teaching guides.

C. Partnering with Institutions

To achieve real scale, we must also bring in **governments, NGOs, universities, and corporations** as partners, not just funders. We will collaborate with ministries of education and culture to **document national history, reprint endangered texts**, and **preserve indigenous languages**.

We will collaborate with universities to translate research into accessible knowledge through **books, courses, guides, and open-access papers.**

We will support NGOs in turning their impact into tools**, lessons learned, case studies, and community stories.** We will also invite the private sector to offer publishing scholarships, grants, and mentorships to underserved voices.

This multi-sector partnership is key to ensuring that publishing becomes a **development strategy**, not just an artistic pursuit.

D. Creating a Pan-African Publishing Marketplace

Finally, all this content, once created, needs a place to live, grow, and generate value. That's why we are building a **digital publishing marketplace** focused on African stories, voices, and knowledge products.

This platform will do more than sell books. It will host:

- E-books and audiobooks
- Online courses based on African knowledge

- Licensable documentaries, films, and animations
- Cultural merchandise, journals, and language tools
- Curriculum materials for schools written by African educators

It will enable diaspora communities to support local creatives, sponsor projects, and reconnect with their roots through storytelling. It will enable schools and universities to access **localised content, teachers to find culturally aligned materials, and entrepreneurs to monetise their knowledge.**

This is not just e-commerce. This is **economic and cultural self-determination.**

Publishing Africa at scale means moving from isolated efforts to **a coordinated ecosystem,** one that stretches from Kampala to Kinshasa, Nairobi to New York, Lagos to London. It means building a continent that not only writes its story, but owns it, protects it, and profits from it.

We are not just printing pages. We are building power.

Why This Model Works for Africa

The Publishing Africa Model was not borrowed from the West. It was born from the realities, rhythms, and richness of Africa itself.

It was crafted through years of listening, really listening to the voices of market vendors, village elders, youth leaders, pastors, teachers, refugees, and returnees. It is a system that works not just in theory, but in practice because it meets people where they are.

It is inclusive.

This model doesn't require a university degree or a publishing background to get started. Whether someone is a school dropout with a lived experience or a professional with decades of wisdom, the process honours their voice.

In Africa, many of our greatest teachers have never stepped into a lecture hall, but their stories can light up generations. This model gives them a path to become published, without gatekeeping or intimidation.

It is affordable.

One of the greatest barriers to publishing in Africa is cost. The traditional model is often expensive and out of reach. That's why we've built low-cost, digital-first pathways that still deliver professional results.

With a smartphone, an Internet connection, and mentorship, anyone can start. We've worked with widows in Uganda and students in Kenya using basic tools, and their books now inspire people worldwide.

It is adaptable.

Whether you are based in Kampala, Kigali, Accra, or Atlanta, the model is designed to fit your context. We've helped Africans in rural villages and diaspora cities alike.

The process works across languages, literacy levels, and lifestyles. It can be used in a group setting in a school or one-on-one with a coach. Whether you're writing a memoir, a manual, a devotional, or a children's book, it flexes to fit the purpose.

It is empowering.

This model is not about printing books. It's about shifting mindsets. We've seen single mothers turn their life lessons into children's books. Farmers turn traditional knowledge into community guides. Survivors of war turn pain into platforms for peace.

People don't just publish, they heal, grow, earn, and lead. A book becomes a business. A story becomes a school. A testimony becomes a tool for transformation. This is the real wealth of publishing.

Above all, it is distinctly African.

The Action Wealth Publishing Model was built to honour oral traditions, not erase them. It embodies our spiritual values, family ties, and community-based approach to learning. It respects our languages, whether Bemba, Swahili, Runyankole, Yoruba, or Krio.

It knows that wisdom doesn't always sit in silence, it dances in drums, flows through proverbs, and speaks through song. That's why this model doesn't try to Westernise publishing, it Africanizes it.

In short, it works because it's ours.

Publishing as an Economic and Social Engine

Publishing is more than printing. It is a force, quiet but mighty, that shapes societies, creates jobs, and builds bridges across generations. Each time an African publishes a book, records a podcast, or shares a story with intention, they are not only preserving memories, but also building an economy and contributing to a collective future.

Every published work has ripple effects. A children's book written in Yoruba helps preserve a language and educate the next generation. A podcast on entrepreneurship in Nairobi may inspire thousands to start businesses.

A grandmother's recipe book becomes not only a family heirloom but a product on the shelves of diaspora supermarkets.

A published life story becomes a mirror for a struggling teenager, a roadmap for an aspiring leader, or a funding tool for a community project.

Publishing preserves culture, yes, but it also informs, uplifts, and employs. With every documented story, we plant seeds of dignity, visibility, and prosperity.

Stories create jobs for editors, designers, voiceover artists, translators, typesetters, marketers, web developers, and printers. One book may involve a dozen professionals, each earning, learning, and growing through that project. But the impact doesn't stop at the individual.

When we scale Publishing Africa across the continent, we do more than help people publish; we build an industry. We create a new class of African content creators. We nurture a generation of African editors, designers, ghostwriters, and publishers. We inspire innovation in language tech, audio content, and education.

And ultimately, we amplify Africa's voice on the global stage not as charity cases, but as creators, contributors, and change agents. Publishing Africa, done intentionally and inclusively, becomes a lever for economic empowerment and social transformation.

This is not a dream. It is already happening story by story, voice by voice, page by page.

What's Next: Building the Infrastructure

Having proven the model across multiple countries and communities, the next phase is scale. However, scale requires infrastructure systems that outlast individuals, platforms that democratise access, and networks that amplify impact.

To publish Africa at scale, we need partners who understand that publishing is not just an artistic venture, but a developmental one. We're seeking those who are willing to invest not only in words, but in the people who carry them.

We are calling for:

- **Scholarships** to equip youth, women, and elders with the skills to document their lives and publish their insights.
- **Publishing hubs** in villages and cities, community spaces with the internet, training, and tools to bring stories to life.
- **Digital platforms** designed for Africa are built to support multilingual content, accessible payment options, local narratives, and global reach.
- **AI-powered transcription and translation tools**, developed with cultural sensitivity, to

convert oral wisdom into searchable, storable, and shareable knowledge.

The model is ready. The blueprint is tested. What we need now is:

- ➢ **Capital** to fuel infrastructure.
- ➢ **Collaboration** with governments, schools, churches, and community groups.
- ➢ **Commitment** from those who understand that documentation is not a luxury, it's a legacy.

We are not looking for saviours. We are building with partners. Together, we can create the tools and systems that empower Africans to write their truth, own their story, and share their voice.

Conclusion: Africa Can Publish Itself Systematically

Africa does not need to wait for foreign publishers, global foundations, or tech platforms to permit us. We already hold the most important ingredients: the stories, the people, and the purpose. What we need now is to structure a system that works at scale, and the courage to use it.

The Publishing Africa Model is proof that Africans can tell their own stories, build their own publishing systems, and profit from their own intellectual property. It's more than a process, it's a promise: that with the right tools and support, we can transform stories into strategies, culture into commerce, and memory into momentum.

Africa doesn't need to be written *about*. Africa needs to be written *by* Africans.

"When we publish our past, we protect our future. When we publish our truth, we create our value."
— **Geoffrey Semaganda.**

This is not about building monuments. This is about building a movement powered by publishing, driven by purpose, and anchored in African pride.

Let the writing continue.

CHAPTER NINE

LEARNING AND MASTERING THE AFRICAN NARRATIVE

"People don't just learn by reading. They learn by hearing, seeing, experiencing, and doing. If we want Africa's stories to stick, we must publish them in the ways people learn."

— **Geoffrey Semaganda.**

Documenting Africa is not enough. To truly reclaim our power, we must ensure that African knowledge is not only preserved but taught, embodied, remembered, and passed on. Publishing is the first step. The next is education. And education must match the rhythm of the people.

Too often, we assume that printing a book or uploading an article is the end of the process. But for a continent built on oral tradition, communal living, apprenticeship, and spiritual symbolism, learning is a layered, experiential journey. Africa's wisdom has always been transmitted through song and story, proverbs and parables, rituals and repetition, not just ink on paper.

If we want Africa's narratives to take root, we must speak to the whole human being: the **eyes**, the **ears**, the **heart**, and the **hands**. We must teach in the languages people speak, using the formats they engage with on a daily basis. We must teach in classrooms and kitchens, in fields and theatres, on stages and smartphones.

The African narrative must not only be read, but it must be lived.

There are five powerful pathways of learning: reading, hearing, seeing, doing, and remembering. Each offers an entry point into how we can make African knowledge unforgettable. Together, they form a blueprint for education that is culturally grounded, emotionally resonant, and generationally sustainable.

We have looked deeply at the first and most familiar: reading, So, let's start this chapter with exploring hearing and listening through a fresh African lens.

Listening: Sound as a Tool for Memory

Africa is, at its core, an oral continent. Long before the printing press or digital screens, knowledge lived in the soundscape of the people carried through drumbeats, chants, praise songs, storytelling circles, and whispered wisdom under starlit skies. The voice was the vessel. The ear was the library.

For generations, we remembered not because we read, but because we listened. Grandmothers spoke in proverbs. Elders retold battles and beginnings. Singers turned histories into melodies. Every village had a voice.

Every fire became a forum. Every drumbeat was both rhythm and record.

Today, we have the tools to preserve this sonic heritage not just as nostalgia, but as a modern publishing strategy. Audio content is more than a trend; it is a return to what has always worked for Africa. It bypasses literacy barriers. It reaches those who have never held a book. It travels faster than paper and lasts longer than memory.

To truly preserve Africa for the ear, we must invest in audio archives that capture the voices of elders before they fall silent. We must empower young people to become skilled journalists, collecting stories from their communities using nothing but a phone and a passion. We must produce podcasts in African languages on topics ranging from spirituality to science, farming to fatherhood. Spoken word artists should be given the same respect as scholars, because they, too, are keepers of knowledge.

Community radio stations, still the heartbeat of many rural regions, must be used not only for news but for cultural education. Imagine a series on the history of African hairstyles. A segment on herbal remedies passed down in Wolof. A nightly story hour for children told by village elders.

Listening is intimate. It's accessible. It's powerful. A grandmother in rural Gambia can transmit life-changing wisdom through a voice note. A Maasai elder can narrate a thousand years of tradition in a single afternoon. And someone halfway across the world can hear it, feel it, and be transformed by it.

When we publish through sound, we ensure that Africa speaks and the world listens.

Watching: Visual Storytelling That Captures the Soul

They say a picture is worth a thousand words. But in Africa, where so many words have been spoken and yet so few recorded, a video can be worth a million. Visual storytelling is not just entertainment, it is education, preservation, empowerment, and identity. It is a mirror, a window, and a bridge all at once.

Africa is a continent rich in visual expression. From our dances to our dress, from our ceremonies to our communal gatherings, our traditions are inherently cinematic. The way a village prepares for a wedding, the rhythm of a drum circle, and the quiet dignity of a funeral rite, all of these are stories worth capturing. And now, we have the tools.

Smartphones, drones, and digital cameras are today's publishing presses. A teenager in Kisumu can film his grandfather explaining how conflicts were resolved without courts. A group of girls in Accra can turn a fable from their grandmother into a short animated film.

A community in Madagascar can document their harvest rituals and upload them to YouTube for the world to witness. These are not just posts, they are publications. They are living archives.

To visually preserve the African narrative, we must be intentional. We must film our traditional dances, not as curiosities for tourists but as cultural textbooks for our children. We must produce documentaries that go beyond slavery and struggle, highlighting untold histories, unsung heroes, and current changemakers. We must encourage TikTok and Instagram content that reflects our values, languages, and realities, not just imported trends.

Visual learning cuts across literacy barriers and generational divides. A child may not read a textbook about the kingdoms of Mali, but he will remember the animation that showed Mansa Musa riding through the desert with caravans of gold. A mother may not attend a workshop on maternal health, but she will watch a WhatsApp video in her language on postpartum care.

It's about seeing ourselves and seeing each other. When a Luo child watches a Ganda rite of passage, or when a Senegalese youth discovers Ethiopian script in a subtitled video, we build continental consciousness. We create unity without uniformity.

When Africans see their language, their skin, their humour, and their history on screen, they are affirmed. Their reality is validated. Their future is reimagined. Visual publishing is not a luxury. It is a necessity. It is how we capture the soul of Africa and share it with the world.

Experiencing: Learning Through Interaction

True learning rarely happens in isolation. In African tradition, wisdom was not simply taught, it was lived. Lessons were absorbed around the fire, in the fields, during ceremonies, and through communal dialogue. Knowledge was not delivered through lectures; it was embedded in experience.

If we are to preserve and transmit the African narrative effectively, we must reclaim this way of learning through doing, seeing, hearing, and feeling.

Experiential learning, the kind that happens through participation, not just observation, is a powerful and often underutilised tool. It allows people to internalise values, understand history, and connect with their identity in tangible ways. Imagine a child who doesn't just read about their tribe's origin story but hears it directly from a village elder, dressed in full regalia, during a storytelling circle at school. That story doesn't just stay in their head. It lives in their heart.

To institutionalise this kind of learning, we need to create environments where African heritage is not only told but also touched, tasted, and tried. Heritage museums and cultural centres should be established in every region, serving not only as archives but also as interactive classrooms. Schools should integrate community publishing camps where students gather oral histories, document local proverbs, and present them in creative formats from plays to digital exhibits.

Even technology has a role here. Imagine simulation games that teach youth how ancient African societies governed themselves, resolved conflict, or traded across regions. These tools bring forgotten wisdom back to life and make it relevant for today.

Churches, mosques, and community centres can become spaces for intergenerational storytelling, where elders share and youth record, perform, and publish. Young people can be encouraged to interview family members, trace their ancestry, and present their findings not just as academic assignments, but as personal discoveries. Every community can host storytelling festivals, arts residencies, and "culture camps" that bridge the gap between oral tradition and modern expression.

Because here's the truth: people remember what they experience. A person who watches a video may be inspired. But a person who reenacts a ritual, cooks a traditional meal with their grandmother, or walks the path of their ancestors in a historical reenactment will never forget it. That kind of learning is embodied. It goes deeper than theory or facts.

Experiential learning is how Africa has always taught. And it is how Africa must teach again. If we want our stories to be remembered, not just heard, we must make them unforgettable.

Mastering: Teaching to Transform

True mastery is not about how much you know, it's about how well you can pass that knowledge on. In African culture, this has always been clear. Elders were not revered for simply knowing stories, but for their ability to tell them. A healer wasn't respected just for knowing herbs, but for how they taught others to apply them. A master drummer wasn't honoured merely for his skill, but for how he trained the next generation of rhythm keepers.

Teaching is the ultimate expression of learning. It requires ownership of knowledge, emotional intelligence, and the willingness to serve others. When someone becomes a teacher, whether formally in a classroom or informally as a community mentor, they become a vessel through which culture flows, evolves, and survives.

To truly publish Africa, we must move beyond content creation and into capacity building. We need to train documentation mentors and publishing ambassadors who can work at the grassroots level to support the community.

These individuals should be equipped not just with technical tools like writing, recording, or editing, but also with cultural sensitivity, listening skills, and a passion for preservation.

African Studies programs must be redesigned to go beyond history and anthropology, and instead prepare educators, artists, and leaders to teach Africa's stories in modern, engaging, and multi-sensory ways. Certification programs can be developed for oral historians, translators, cultural coaches, and even local archivists. These are the people who will carry the torch, community by community, generation by generation.

The African diaspora plays a critical role in this ecosystem. We must encourage African professionals abroad, authors, pastors, scholars, activists, and entrepreneurs to mentor youth back home in the art of documentation and storytelling. Through digital platforms, mentorship circles, and exchange programs, the diaspora can help reinforce cultural pride and publishing skills where they are most needed.

In a world where algorithms and AI are flattening cultures, we need living archives people who not only hold Africa's story but also embody it. Every town, village, and diaspora network should have such people: women and men who carry, teach, and expand the African narrative with love, skill, and responsibility.

Because when someone teaches, they do not just transmit knowledge, they transform identity. And in the transformation of identity, a continent rises.

Building Learning Ecosystems

To truly embed the African narrative into our lives and future, it's not enough to produce content; we must design ecosystems that support lifelong, multi-sensory learning. Each of the five learning pathways reading, listening, watching, experiencing, and mastering can only flourish when nurtured within intentional environments. These are not just classrooms. They are creative spaces, cultural centres, homes, and digital platforms where knowledge is not just taught, but lived.

Imagine heritage learning centres in rural communities where children can hear stories in their native tongues, learn traditional crafts, and trace their ancestry through local archives. In urban schools, tech-enabled classrooms could double as publishing labs where students write blogs, produce podcasts, create animated folktales, or publish youth magazines. Universities could house podcast and video studios, enabling academic knowledge to be transformed into accessible public education.

We must cultivate intergenerational mentorship, deliberately pairing youth with elders so that wisdom can be transferred not just through theory, but through genuine relationships. Whether it's a teenager recording their grandmother's recipe or a student learning indigenous conflict resolution from a retired chief, this kind of learning is priceless.

In the digital space, we can unify these methods. Imagine a Pan-African digital platform that blends books, videos, podcasts, and discussions all in multiple languages, designed for various literacy levels, and open to the world. A platform where an African in Accra, a student in Atlanta, and a healer in Kisumu can learn from one another.

These ecosystems must be as diverse as our continent and as inclusive as our traditions. They should reflect local realities while contributing to a shared Pan-African vision because the goal is not just to preserve knowledge, but to pass it on in ways that are relevant, relational, and resilient.

Publishing without pedagogy is noise. But when we build intentional learning ecosystems, Africa's knowledge becomes a living, growing, liberating force.

Using Festivals, Schools, and Faith Centres

To truly reclaim and master the African narrative, we must meet people where they are not just in academic halls or official archives, but in the vibrant, everyday spaces where African life unfolds.

Schools, for instance, should not limit learning to textbook knowledge. Every subject, such as math, history, agriculture, or literature, can include publishing exercises. A biology student might document traditional medicinal plants used in their village. A literature class might collect and publish local folktales. In doing so, education becomes a tool not just for exams, but for preservation.

Faith centres, churches, mosques, temples, and traditional spiritual spaces can play an equally vital role. These institutions already shape values and identity for millions across the continent.

By encouraging documentation of African theological thought, contextual sermons, and spiritual encounters, they preserve a faith that is rooted in the African soil, not borrowed from abroad. Pastors, imams, and elders can publish devotionals, testimonies, and reflections in local languages, affirming that God also speaks through African experience.

Festivals, too, are more than celebrations; they are cultural classrooms. At music, dance, and food festivals, we can showcase documented traditions. We can set up storytelling booths, oral history tents, and local author showcases. Cultural preservation doesn't need to be hidden in museums; it can be expressed through singing, dancing, and served on a plate.

Even in markets, Africa's economic nerve centres can become unlikely distribution points for cultural products. Books by local writers, audio stories on flash drives, or educational posters can be sold alongside vegetables and spices, reaching those who may never step into a bookstore.

And then there's the home, the most sacred learning space of all. Imagine every African child growing up with a personal library shelf filled not with Western fairy tales alone, but with stories written by their own family: a father's memoir, a grandmother's recipe book, a family tree bound in print.

When publishing becomes integrated into our lifestyle, not just our schooling, we create a living culture of knowledge. A society where storytelling is not an event, but a way of life. Where memory is honoured, and identity is reinforced every day, in every place, by everyone.

Monitoring and Celebrating Progress

For Africa to truly master its narrative, documentation must not be a one-off project; it must become a lifestyle, a system, and a movement. And like any movement worth sustaining, it needs to be measured, tracked, and celebrated.

We must start by monitoring what's being produced using these guiding questions:

- ➤ How many books were published in Swahili this year?
- ➤ How many testimonies or elders were recorded in northern Uganda?
- ➤ How many podcasts in Yoruba, films in Amharic, or children's books in isiZulu were uploaded online?

These are indicators of cultural health and national identity.

Understanding that metrics alone aren't enough, we must also celebrate. Imagine national awards for village authors, schoolchildren who publish their first community story, or the 100th traditional healer whose knowledge has been preserved in audio or video format. Milestones matter; they build morale, inspire others, and remind us that our efforts are not in vain.

Scholarships and grants should be awarded to those actively documenting their communities, whether it's a grandmother compiling recipes, a youth leader filming community tradition, or a teacher transcribing oral proverbs. These culture keepers are not just storytellers; they are the historians of our time.

To tie it all together, we must establish a continental framework and a yearly *African Story Index*. This index would document the growth of our publishing efforts, highlight key contributors, and provide a clear picture of how Africa is reclaiming its voice, region by region, language by language, medium by medium.

What gets measured gets managed. But more important, what gets celebrated gets repeated. And Africa needs this rhythm of remembrance and recognition to fuel its renaissance.

Conclusion: Teach Africa to Learn from Itself

Africa does not need to import identity. It needs to remember, retell, and relearn who it truly is. To publish Africa is to document it. But to master Africa is to teach it to embed its stories, truths, and visions into every home, every classroom, every sermon, every song, and every screen.

This is not just about learning in the traditional sense. This is about teaching Africa to learn itself through reading, listening, watching, experiencing, and mentoring.

Through every sense. Every generation. Every community.

When an African child reads of her ancestors, when a young man in the diaspora listens to his grandmother's voice telling a proverb, when a teacher turns storytelling into a subject, when a TikTok skit explains a forgotten ritual, something powerful happens.

Africa begins to remember. And when Africa learns itself wholly, richly, truthfully, it can never again be erased.

"When Africa learns itself through every sense, every channel, every generation, we will never again be forgotten."

— **Geoffrey Semaganda.**

This is more than a publishing campaign. This is the education of a continent into its greatness.

Let us not just tell Africa's story. Let us live it. Teach it. Master it

CHAPTER TEN

A CALL TO FUND AFRICA'S STORY

"The cost of not funding documentation is greater than the cost of funding it. If we do not invest in our memory, we invest in our disappearance."
— **Geoffrey Semaganda**

Publishing Africa is not a poetic dream. It is a strategic necessity. And like every meaningful transformation, it demands investment not just in vision, but in infrastructure, systems, and people.

For too long, documentation and cultural preservation have been treated as afterthoughts, nice-to-haves rather than must-haves. Ministries of Culture are often among the least funded in national budgets. Artists, authors, and archivists work with little to no support. National libraries decay. Museums go unvisited.

Traditional knowledge carriers grow old without ever having their wisdom recorded. Meanwhile, millions of young Africans walk around with powerful digital tools in their pockets but lack the training or platforms to publish their stories, document their discoveries, or monetise their creativity.

This chapter is not just a call to action; it is a *call for financing*. Because the truth is uncomfortable but clear: if Africa does not fund its own story, no one else will. If we do not prioritise our voice, our memory, and our identity, they will continue to be overwritten by others. And the cost of that erasure is far greater than the price of preservation.

The Funding Gap: A Hidden Crisis

Across the continent, billions of dollars are allocated each year to roads, power plants, and other physical infrastructure. Security budgets grow. Humanitarian funding flows. Conferences are hosted.

However, the amount set aside for cultural production, publishing, and content creation is shockingly low, often buried under miscellaneous development categories or at the mercy of donor whims.

And yet, without the story, none of the structures matter.

- ✧ What good is a highway if the culture it connects is forgotten?
- ✧ What use is a government policy if it is undocumented, unread, or untranslatable?
- ✧ How far can a community go if it does not remember where it came from?

Documentation is the infrastructure of the soul. It gives shape to memory, continuity to ideas, and resilience to identity. It enables evaluation, replication, and learning.

It turns personal sacrifice into national wisdom, and collective pain into global lessons.

But for this to happen, funding must be intentional and visible. The lack of it is not just an inconvenience; it is a crisis. It means generations of ideas die in silence. It means indigenous science is lost to memory. It means African children grow up with no books that reflect their faces, names, or ancestors.

This is not just a cultural issue, it is an economic, social, and political issue. Africa's under-documentation is not accidental; it is a result of strategic underfunding. And if we are serious about changing this, we *must treat publishing and preservation with the same urgency* as we do food, roads, and other essential services.

Because, in the long run, our ability to build nations depends not only on what we construct, but on what we remember.

Why Fund Publishing? Seven Reasons That Matter

Investing in publishing is not just about printing books, it is about securing Africa's future across every sector, from education to economics, identity to innovation.

Here are seven critical reasons why funding publishing must become a continental priority:

1. **First, preservation.** Every culture, language, proverb, and ritual that is documented stands a chance of survival. Every oral history captured, every ancestral teaching recorded, is a victory against extinction.

Funding documentation is how we preserve the irreplaceable. Without it, the treasures of our past vanish with each passing generation.

2. **Second, education.** When we fund publishing, we fund African learning materials, textbooks that reflect our histories, storybooks that elevate our heroes, podcasts that unpack local challenges, and courses that teach from an African worldview.

   Without publishing, education becomes disconnected from our reality, reinforcing colonial narratives instead of empowering students to think with context and pride.

3. **Third, the economy.** A well-funded publishing industry stimulates job creation across the creative and intellectual spectrum. Writers, editors, illustrators, translators, printers, software developers, voiceover artists, and cultural researchers all benefit from this collaboration.

   These are not just jobs. They are careers that help build a new knowledge economy rooted in African voices.

4. **Fourth, tourism.** No tourist is drawn to silence. They come for the stories, the history, the art, the music, and the soul of a place. Countries that invest in cultural documentation reap the benefits of cultural tourism.

   Africa has a rich heritage that, without documentation, much of it remains hidden, inaccessible, or misunderstood.

5. **Fifth, innovation.** Indigenous knowledge systems contain remarkable insights into sustainable agriculture, community health, governance, and conflict resolution. But unless these systems are documented, studied, and shared, they cannot inform or inspire modern solutions. Funding publishing means funding innovation that is born from our roots.
6. **Sixth, identity.** Publishing affirms who we are. It reclaims pride in being African. It breaks the cycle of shame and inferiority that colonialism, slavery, and misrepresentation have left behind. When we see our stories told by us, for us, we remember that our identity is not a burden, it is a beacon.
7. **Seventh, and perhaps most urgent of all, AI readiness.** As artificial intelligence becomes the filter through which the world accesses information, only those who have documented their knowledge will be represented in its databases. If we fail to publish, Africa will be digitally invisible, excluded from future platforms, policies, and perceptions.

In short, funding publishing is not just an act of cultural love, it is a strategic investment. It touches every part of national development.

It is time Africa stops treating publishing as a luxury and starts treating it as a national security issue.

Who Must Fund the Story? Everyone.

Funding Africa's story is not the job of one government, one agency, or one donor. It is a shared responsibility because the story belongs to all of us. The survival and rise of the African narrative must be funded by every sector that benefits from its richness, wisdom, and potential.

Here's how different stakeholders must play their part:

- **Governments** must lead by example. They must allocate real, not symbolic, budgets for cultural documentation, the development of educational content, and the preservation of national memory through public archives. Ministries of Culture, Education, and Information must be empowered and equipped.

    National publishing boards and copyright offices need sustainable funding to support writers, protect intellectual property, and distribute African stories across borders. Grants should be made available to authors, local publishers, cultural institutions, and grassroots storytellers to tell the stories that matter most.

- **Philanthropists and impact investors** must see publishing as a purpose-driven investment. Storytelling and cultural preservation should be treated as vital forms of social impact.

    Philanthropic capital can sponsor publishing accelerators, creative fellowships, and youth-led storytelling projects. Impact funds should support

African media startups, local language platforms, and content creation labs for women and marginalised voices. This is not charity, it's capacity building.

✧ **The African diaspora** must become custodians of cultural continuity. They can establish heritage funds to support publishing in their home communities, sponsor storytelling competitions, and equip libraries and schools with culturally relevant books and media.

Beyond funding, diaspora communities can co-author stories, record oral history from their parents and grandparents, and mentor local storytellers to bring global publishing knowledge back home.

✧ **NGOs and development agencies** must integrate documentation into their core programs. Whether working in health, education, gender, or agriculture, these agencies should include cultural knowledge publishing as part of their capacity-building frameworks.

Every project has a story, and every intervention has a lesson worth recording. They should fund translations, invest in local language media, and require documentation of impact in culturally sensitive ways.

✧ **The private sector** must see publishing as good business. Through corporate social responsibility (CSR), companies can support storytelling initiatives that uplift the communities they serve. They can sponsor the documentation of local histories, oral traditions, and success stories.

In doing so, they strengthen their brand while contributing to the preservation of culture. Businesses can also document their own histories, creating books and media that highlight African innovation and entrepreneurial journeys.

- **Faith institutions** must document their divine assignments. Churches, mosques, temples, and traditional spiritual houses carry immense moral influence. Yet many do not preserve their histories, teachings, or testimonies.

  These institutions must establish publishing departments that record spiritual experiences, translate sacred texts into African languages, and publish theology contextualised for African realities. They must equip their members to tell stories of faith, struggle, healing, and transformation in a way that resonates across generations.

The truth is, no one is exempt. If you benefit from Africa's wisdom, beauty, talent, or spirit, you have a role to play in funding its story because the cost of silence is far greater than the cost of documentation.

How to Fund Strategically

When it comes to documenting and publishing Africa's story, how we fund is just as important as how much we fund. Strategic funding means thinking long-term. It means moving beyond one-off book launches and looking at how to build a publishing ecosystem that can sustain itself, scale across borders, and serve generations.

We must stop treating publishing as an isolated activity and begin funding it as a national, communal, and continental development strategy.

First, fund training, not just output. A published book or recorded documentary is powerful, but its impact multiplies when it sparks a cycle of ongoing creation. That's why funding should begin with people.

We must invest in the writers, editors, translators, designers, animators, and podcasters who will keep telling Africa's stories long after the initial project ends.

This means sponsoring writers' residencies, media training programs, and storytelling academies across the continent. When you train a storyteller, you fund a thousand future stories.

Second, fund infrastructure. Without the physical and digital spaces to create, preserve, and share, even the most talented voices remain unheard. Strategic funding should go toward building and upgrading recording studios, community libraries, digitisation labs, mobile publishing units, and cultural centres.

These are not luxuries; they are the foundation of a publishing ecosystem. Just as we fund roads and hospitals, we must build the spaces where memory is preserved and multiplied.

Third, fund local language content. Africa's diversity is its strength, but it also presents a challenge: stories must be told in many tongues. Strategic funding ensures that rural and indigenous communities are not left behind.

This means supporting translators, voiceover artists, and cultural researchers who can make content available in local dialects. It also means fairly compensating those who hold and transmit cultural knowledge, such as elders and traditional custodians.

Fourth, fund technology. In a digital world, strategic funding must enable Africans to reach the global stage with a single tap of the screen. This includes investing in user-friendly platforms for self-publishing, podcasting, and video distribution. It also means digitising rare manuscripts and historical archives, so they are not lost to time.

Emerging tools, such as blockchain, can be utilised to protect African intellectual property and ensure that creators are properly credited and compensated for their work.

Finally, fund networks, not just individuals. A single author can inspire change, but a collective can sustain it. Funding should support publishing collectives, community writing groups, and networks of storytellers who work together across regions and generations.

These networks foster collaboration, mentorship, cultural exchange, and resource sharing. They also help distribute content more widely and ensure that the movement to publish Africa is not isolated, but connected and continuous.

Strategic funding doesn't just support projects. It builds capacity. It empowers voices. It seeds industries. It creates the conditions for Africa to tell its story again and again louder and stronger each time.

The Publishing Africa Fund: A Vision for Scale

To close the massive gap between Africa's cultural wealth and its documented presence in the world, we must go beyond scattered efforts and isolated projects. We need a continental mechanism visionary in its scope, practical in its function, and transparent in its governance.

That's why we propose the creation of the **Publishing Africa Fund:** a coordinated, pan-African initiative designed to finance the future of our stories.

The Publishing Africa Fund is not just another donor pool; it is a *movement bank*, a structured system to resource the voices, platforms, and infrastructure necessary for Africa to write, record, and broadcast its truth on a global scale. It will combine contributions from governments, philanthropists, diaspora communities, private companies, and international development partners. But more important, it will channel those resources directly into the hands of creators, educators, and cultural custodians.

This fund will support the documentation of endangered languages, forgotten histories, and overlooked oral traditions. It will help build youth-led publishing startups that tell stories in new formats and on new platforms.

It will finance the development of community publishing hubs, mobile recording studios, and digital storytelling centres in both rural and urban Africa. It will underwrite the creation of textbooks rooted in African reality, children's books that reflect African heroes, and media that celebrate African excellence.

But it won't stop at content creation. The Publishing Africa Fund will provide resources for translation and digitisation projects, ensuring accessibility across regions, languages, and technologies. It will invest in human capital by training editors, writers, producers, archivists, animators, and documentary makers. Every funded project will be accompanied by technical mentorship and follow-up support to ensure quality, scalability, and long-term impact.

To guarantee transparency and accountability, the Fund will operate with a clear reporting system that tracks the number of stories published, the communities reached, and the economic outcomes generated. It will offer micro-grants for grassroots projects, seed funding for startups, and larger investments for regional and national initiatives.

Africa has no shortage of stories. What we've lacked is the structure to scale them. **The Publishing Africa Fund is our answer.**

We cannot afford to rely on luck or goodwill. We must build the infrastructure, fund the systems, pay the creators, protect the content, and scale the ecosystem. Anything less is betrayal. Anything less is silence.

The Return on Investment (ROI)

In the world of finance, ROI is a measure of the return on investment, or the amount of gain realised from a specific investment. When it comes to funding Africa's story, the returns are not only financial, but they are also transformational. Every dollar invested in documentation, publishing, and cultural preservation plants a seed whose fruits feed generations.

The cultural return is immediate and profound. A documented story fosters identity, pride, and a sense of belonging. It strengthens the social fabric, reduces conflict born from misunderstanding, and gives communities a shared memory to rally around. In places where stories are told, wars are avoided. When people understand their roots, they are less likely to reject others.

The educational return is generational. A well-funded textbook, a children's story in a local language, or a podcast series on African innovation doesn't expire after one use. These are resources that can teach, inspire, and shape minds for decades. Unlike imported curricula, local content speaks directly to the hearts and contexts of African learners.

The economic return is multifold. Creative industries publishing, media, film, design, and audio production become engines of employment and enterprise. A thriving publishing ecosystem supports writers, editors, illustrators, printers, distributors, and digital platforms. It turns knowledge into jobs and stories into income.

The global return is equally powerful. A well-documented culture attracts curiosity. It boosts tourism, invites trade, and shifts global perceptions. It gives Africa a voice not only in politics and business but in how the world imagines, remembers, and includes us.

The digital return on the AI dividend is the most urgent. In an age where machines learn from what's documented, every story we fund feeds the algorithmic memory of the future. If Africa is not published, it will be excluded. But when we invest in our voice, we shape how the world and the machines that power it see us, treat us, and interact with us.

Documentation is not a sunk cost. It is a rising asset. A multiplier. A generator of wealth, wisdom, and world-changing influence.

What You Can Do Now

The task of funding Africa's story may sound massive, but it begins with simple, intentional actions. Everyone, no matter their position, profession, or postcode, has a role to play in preserving the soul of the continent.

You don't have to build a library or fund an entire film to make a difference. Sometimes, the spark that lights the flame is small but powerful.

- **Sponsor a storyteller.** Find someone in your village, church, or circle who holds valuable memories: an elder, a war survivor, a healer, a farmer and pay for them to record their story. Whether through writing, audio, or video, that story could become a source of pride and learning for generations to come.
- **Buy African books.** Put your money where your mouth is. When you purchase stories written by

African authors, you fuel a market, you create demand, and you prove that there is value in our voices.
- **Donate to heritage funds.** Join the collective effort to safeguard culture by supporting organisations and initiatives that are preserving language, land, rituals, and history.
- **Mentor a young person.** Whether you're a writer, a teacher, or simply someone with a phone and internet access, help a young African document their story. Guide them through the process. Encourage them to see the worth in their words.
- **Partner with us.** At Publishing Africa, we are building systems to make publishing scalable, accessible, and sustainable. Whether you want to fund a hub, sponsor a book, or bring publishing training to your region, we invite you to collaborate.

Even a single act, say the printing of one book, the translation of one proverb, or the digitisation of one archive, can ripple through time.

Conclusion: We Cannot Afford Silence

Silence is not neutral. It is not passive. In the African context, silence has become a slow erasure not because our ancestors were quiet, not because our communities lack culture, but because the world has failed to invest in their voices. And because we too often have failed to invest in our own.

The silence of Africa is not a reflection of its emptiness; it is a reflection of underinvestment.

We cannot afford that silence any longer. The cost is too high.

We must fund the scribes, the archivists, the poets, the healers, the digital creators, and the village historians. We must invest in the platforms, tools, translations, and training. We must support the storytellers as if our future depends on it because it does.

A story told is a legacy secured.

A story funded is a future insured.

Let's not just preserve our past, let's pay forward our memory.

Let's fund the future of Africa's voice.

CHAPTER ELEVEN

THE FUTURE STARTS WITH OUR STORY

"Africa's future will not be written by chance. It must be written by choice."
— **Geoffrey Semaganda**

A Call Beyond Ourselves

This is the beginning of a new history. A history not written by outsiders or assumed by algorithms, but authored by us, in our voices, with our truths.

Africa today stands at a crossroads. On one side lies silence, erasure, and dependence, a future where others continue to describe us, define us, and design solutions for us. On the other side lies voice, memory, and power, a future where we take ownership of our past, our present, and our future through the simple yet profound act of publishing.

Publishing is not just about books; it is about survival. In the age of artificial intelligence, what is not documented will not exist. AI does not invent knowledge; it feeds on what has already been written. If Africa's contribution to the global body of published knowledge remains at a mere 2%, then 98% of the data shaping global systems will be defined by voices outside our continent. That means policy, economics, education, and even culture will continue to be explained without us, or worse, misrepresented in ways that diminish us.

We cannot allow this. We must not. The battle for Africa's future is the battle for its memory, and memory is recorded in words, ideas, and stories. The nations that dominate the world are the nations that document it. They record their history, publish their research, preserve their culture, and distribute their knowledge in formats the future can use.

If Africa does not do the same, we will be locked out of the archives of humanity's progress. But if we rise to the challenge, we will not only protect our identity, but also project it.

The Reality Check: Africa at 2%

The global publishing industry produces between three to four million new titles every single year. In comparison, Africa contributes barely 50,000 to 60,000 titles annually across its entire continent. That is less than 2% of the world's total published content.

This is not because Africa lacks stories, creativity, or knowledge. It is because we have not yet built publishing into the core of our development, our identity, and our future. Too often, our knowledge remains trapped in oral form, in scattered papers, or in the memories of elders. Too often, we rely on foreign publishers to validate what we produce, leaving vast amounts of African wisdom undocumented.

The consequences are severe. When Africa is missing from the world's bookshelves, it is missing from research databases. When it is missing from databases, it is missing from artificial intelligence. When it is missing from AI, it is missing from the systems that will govern the future of finance, healthcare, technology, and education.

To remain at 2% is to be invisible in the future of knowledge. And invisibility is the deepest form of disempowerment.

However, the numbers also carry a message of hope. For if we understand the scale of the gap, we can also see the scale of the opportunity. Africa has 1.4 billion people. If just one in 3,000 Africans produced a single book in a year, we would generate nearly half a million new titles. That would catapult us from 2% to 20% of global publishing output, placing us at the centre of global knowledge creation.

This is not impossible. It is within reach. And it begins with each of us.

The Big Goal: From 2% to 20%

If Africa is to claim its rightful place in the future of knowledge, we cannot remain satisfied with 2%. Our goal must be clear and unapologetic: to grow Africa's publishing share to 20% of global output.

That means half a million new African titles every single year on top of what already exists. To some, that number sounds overwhelming. But when you break it down, it becomes both practical and possible.

Think of it this way: the global system already produces three million books a year. Africa, with its 1.4 billion people, currently produces around 50–60,000. To rise to 500,000 is not a fantasy. It is simply a matter of mobilising all sectors of society, individuals, schools, universities, governments, faith institutions, corporations, and the diaspora to each carry their share of the load.

Imagine if every village in Africa produced one author each year. Imagine if every secondary school published an anthology of student writing or a record of community history.

Imagine if every government ministry commissioned books on its policies, languages, and cultural archives. Imagine if every major corporation funded children's literacy projects or industry guides as part of its corporate responsibility.

Imagine if the African diaspora, 200 million strong, committed to documenting its migration stories and lessons.

Suddenly, the impossible begins to look inevitable.

Let's do the mathematics clearly:

- ◆ **Individuals:** With a population of 1.4 billion, if just one in 10,000 Africans publishes a book each year, that alone creates 140,000 books. If one in 3,000 does, we will have crossed 450,000.
- ◆ **Universities:** Africa has over 1,500 universities. If each publisher were to publish just 20 titles annually, including research papers, textbooks, and

local studies, that would add up to 30,000 new books.

✧ **Schools:** There are around 500,000 secondary schools. If just 10% of them (50,000 schools) published two anthologies per year, that is another 100,000 titles.

✧ **Governments:** With 54 African governments, if each sponsored 2,000 titles a year, policy papers, cultural histories, tribal language texts, that adds 108,000.

✧ **Faith Institutions:** If 5,000 churches, mosques, temples, and councils produced 10 titles per year, that is 50,000.

✧ **Diaspora:** With 200 million Africans abroad, if one in every 5,000 published a book annually, that adds 40,000.

✧ **Corporations:** If just 1,000 companies each sponsored 100 titles per year, that adds 100,000.

When you total these contributions, the number easily surpasses 500,000 new African titles per year.

This shows one thing clearly: **no single group can do it alone. But if everyone contributes modestly, the continental target is within reach.**

And why aim for 20%? Because numbers matter. In global debates, visibility is power. When Africa publishes half a million books a year, the continent is no longer a footnote in the archives of knowledge; it becomes a dominant voice.

That means our children will grow up surrounded by stories that reflect their own experiences, identities, and realities. It means that when AI models are trained, they will learn from African languages, African contexts, and African wisdom, not just imported narratives.

20% is not just a publishing target. It is a survival target. It is a power target. It is a dignity target. And it is a future target.

This is the big goal. And now the question becomes: how do we get there, and what's in it for each of us?

INDIVIDUALS:

The Power of One as an Author of Change

When most people think of publishing, they often envision famous writers, academics, or politicians. But in truth, the foundation of Africa's publishing future rests on ordinary people, farmers, teachers, mothers, traders, youth, and elders who each hold knowledge worth recording.

Africa has 1.4 billion people. That is 1.4 billion unique stories, experiences, lessons, and innovations. Yet the majority of these stories are undocumented. A grandmother's proverbs vanish when she passes away. A farmer's method of surviving drought is lost when it is not written down. A young entrepreneur's lessons remain locked in his mind.

Publishing gives permanence to these truths. A single book can carry a life's wisdom across centuries.

What Can Individuals Do?

- ✓ Write personal memoirs, family histories, or community chronicles.
- ✓ Record traditional recipes, farming techniques, or crafts.
- ✓ Publish poetry, short stories, or reflections that preserve culture.
- ✓ Collaborate with others to produce anthologies of local voices.
- ✓ Share professional expertise, whether in business, health, or leadership, in accessible guides.

What Are the Benefits?

- ➢ **Legacy:** Your story becomes part of your family's inheritance. Generations to come will know who you were and what you stood for.
- ➢ **Visibility:** Publishing transforms your knowledge from a private resource into a public contribution. You gain recognition as an authority in your field or as a custodian of your community's wisdom.
- ➢ **Economic Opportunity:** A book can be your No. 1 marketing and income-generating tool. It can create multiple streams of income, open doors to speaking engagements, and build trust, authority, credibility, and influence in the marketplace.
- ➢ **Confidence:** Seeing one's words in print builds pride, especially for youth who realise their voices matter.

> **Contribution to Africa:** Each book adds a brick to the continental library of knowledge. Every individual who publishes expands Africa's presence in global memory.

Imagine This

A retired nurse in Ghana documents her experiences with community health practices. That book becomes a guide for young health workers across West Africa.

A group of teenagers in Uganda publish a poetry anthology about climate change in their village, which travels across schools, inspiring youth activism.

A taxi driver in South Africa documents stories of the people he has driven, the result is a social history richer than any official statistics.

These may sound small, but multiplied across millions of individuals, they become the backbone of Africa's publishing revolution.

If one in every 3,000 Africans published just one book in a year, Africa would already cross 450,000 new titles. That is the power of the individual voice. And that is the responsibility of each of us.

SCHOOLS & UNIVERSITIES:

Knowledge that Builds Futures

Education has always been one of Africa's greatest investments. Our schools and universities are not just places of instruction; they are vaults of untapped knowledge. Every classroom carries research, creativity, culture, and innovation that rarely make it beyond exam papers and dusty archives.

If we want to reach half a million titles a year, our schools and universities must become engines of publishing.

Imagine if every secondary school produced one anthology of student writing or community history per year. Imagine if every university documented its research into textbooks, case studies, and policy reports. The scale would be transformative.

What Can Schools & Universities Do?

Secondary Schools:
- ✓ Publish anthologies of student poems, essays, and oral histories.
- ✓ Record local histories, traditions, and community experiences in simple books.
- ✓ Create guides on social issues written by students for students.

UNIVERSITIES:
- ✓ Turn academic research into accessible books for communities and industries.
- ✓ Publish textbooks written from African contexts rather than imported ones.
- ✓ Document local languages, indigenous knowledge systems, and case studies.
- ✓ Encourage every department to publish annually as part of its academic mandate.

What Are the Benefits?

- **Identity in Education:** Students grow up reading materials that reflect their own contexts, not just foreign examples. A Nigerian student should study economics from Nigerian case studies, not only European ones.
- **Confidence & Pride:** When schools publish student anthologies, young people learn that their voices matter. It builds self-esteem and motivates excellence.
- **Global Recognition:** Universities that publish consistently gain visibility, citations, and influence in global academic discussions. African research enters the world stage.
- **Preservation:** Publishing school histories and local knowledge ensures that traditions, languages, and experiences are not lost but recorded for future generations.
- **Revenue & Sustainability:** Universities and schools can generate income by selling textbooks, manuals, and guides regionally, reducing dependence on imported content.

Imagine This!

A secondary school in rural Kenya publishes a book of student essays about climate change. Within a year, it will be used as a teaching tool across the district.

A university in Nigeria publishes a casebook on African business models, which becomes a required reference in MBA programs worldwide.

A Tanzanian college documents herbal medicine traditions in Swahili and English, preserving them before they disappear and giving rise to new fields of research.

Now multiply this. Africa has over **500,000 secondary schools** and **1,500 universities**. If just 10% of schools published two anthologies annually, that would add 100,000 books. If each university published 20 titles, that would add 30,000 more. Combined, schools and universities alone could contribute 130,000 titles each year, nearly a quarter of the total needed.

But beyond numbers, the real gain is that education becomes rooted in African soil. Our children learn not just about Shakespeare, Newton, or Napoleon but about Okot p'Bitek, Wangari Maathai, and the wisdom of their own ancestors. Publishing transforms education from imitation into innovation.

GOVERNMENTS:

Documentation as National Security

Governments are the custodians of a nation's memory. Within their ministries, archives, and departments lie thousands of documents, histories, policies, cultural records, and research that often remain unpublished or inaccessible to citizens. Too often, valuable national knowledge is scattered across filing cabinets, lost when leaders change, or destroyed by neglect.

Publishing is not just a cultural duty for governments; it is a matter of national security. What is undocumented can be disputed, stolen, or forgotten. Land rights, cultural identities, indigenous languages, and even political histories can vanish if they are not preserved in books, records, and digital archives.

What Can Governments Do?

- ✓ **Commission & Sponsor Publications:** Each ministry should sponsor annual publications, whether policy guides, tribal histories, or research reports.
- ✓ **Support Tribal & Indigenous Languages:** Fund translations, grammar books, and story collections for every African language, ensuring none are lost.
- ✓ **Digitise Archives: National libraries and archives should systematically digitise** old documents, manuscripts, and rare books.
- ✓ **Mandate Educational Content:** Ministries of Education can ensure that schoolbooks are written and published locally, reflecting national realities.
- ✓ **Public Service Publishing Units:** Governments can set up publishing departments that work alongside communities, universities, and researchers to turn raw information into books.

What Are the Benefits?

- ➢ **National Security:** Documented history and land rights reduce conflicts and safeguard national identity. Disputes over borders, resources, or cultural ownership can be resolved with written proof.

- **Cultural Pride:** When governments sponsor tribal histories and language texts, they validate citizens' identities and strengthen unity.
- **Transparency:** Publishing policy documents and development plans increases accountability and citizen participation.
- **Tourism & Diplomacy:** Countries that publish their cultural heritage attract global interest, visitors, and investment.
- **Global Influence:** Nations that publish their research and policies shape international debates, rather than being shaped by them.

Imagine This

Uganda commissions and publishes 500 books on its tribal languages, ensuring no dialect is lost to time.

Nigeria's Ministry of Education develops locally written textbooks for every subject, cutting dependence on imports.

Ghana digitises its national archives, making centuries of history available worldwide at the click of a button.

South Africa publishes detailed policy handbooks on renewable energy, which are cited globally as models for developing economies.

Now imagine this across 54 nations. If each African government were to commit to sponsoring **2,000 titles**

per year, we would generate **108,000 books annually**. That contribution alone would cover more than 20% of the continental target.

But more importantly, governments would be preserving their sovereignty in the digital age. Because without documentation, sovereignty is fragile. A country that does not record its history leaves room for others to rewrite its story.

Publishing, therefore, is not just about knowledge, it is about power. And no African government can afford to neglect it.

CORPORATIONS & INDUSTRY:
Publishing as Legacy and CSR

Africa's private sector is booming. From banks and telecom companies to agribusinesses, mining giants, and tech startups, corporations play a massive role in shaping the continent's present and future. Yet too often, their impact is measured only in profits and quarterly reports.

What if corporations became champions of publishing? What if industry knowledge, best practices, and social responsibility projects were consistently turned into books, guides, and children's stories? The effect would ripple far beyond shareholders... It would shape generations.

Publishing is not a cost. It is an investment in brand, in legacy, and in literacy.

What Can Corporations Do?

- ✓ **Industry Guides:** Publish handbooks, case studies, and manuals relevant to their sector, finance, farming, mining, health, and technology.
- ✓ **Children's Literacy Projects:** Fund and publish storybooks for schools, written in local languages, to promote literacy.
- ✓ **Annual Reports as Knowledge Products:** Transform CSR and sustainability reports into educational materials accessible to the public.
- ✓ **Employee Knowledge Archives:** Encourage staff to co-author anthologies of lessons learned, innovation stories, or community impact.
- ✓ **Partnership Publishing:** Collaborate with NGOs, schools, or faith institutions to co-publish socially impactful content.

What Are the Benefits?

- ➤ **Stronger Brand Trust:** Companies that publish literacy and knowledge resources earn goodwill from communities. A bank that funds financial literacy books creates loyal future customers.
- ➤ **Market Growth:** A literate population is also an empowered consumer base. Publishing literacy materials directly grows the market.
- ➤ **Thought Leadership:** Industry guides position companies as authoritative voices in their fields, shaping both national and global conversations.

- ➢ **CSR with Lasting Impact:** Sponsoring a book lasts far longer than a billboard. It plants seeds of knowledge that influence generations.
- ➢ **Employee Pride & Retention:** Workers who see their contributions documented feel valued, boosting morale and loyalty.

Imagine This

A telecom company in Kenya sponsors 100 children's books in Kiswahili about technology and innovation, distributing them free to schools, shaping a generation of digital thinkers.

A Nigerian bank funds financial literacy manuals written in local dialects, empowering rural communities to save and invest.

A mining company in Zambia publishes community histories of the regions where it operates, preserving culture while improving relations with locals.

A pan-African airline releases an anthology of African travel stories, positioning itself as more than a transporter, it becomes a cultural ambassador.

Now imagine 1,000 corporations across Africa, each sponsoring **100 titles a year**. That alone would contribute **100,000 new books annually**.

But more importantly, it would create an ecosystem where knowledge and commerce feed each other. Corporations would no longer extract value from communities; they would return value in the form of documented wisdom, literacy, and empowerment.

When future generations look back, they will not remember a telecom company for its data bundles or a bank for its interest rates. They will remember the books it sponsored, the knowledge it preserved, and the literacy it spread. That is corporate legacy.

FAITH INSTITUTIONS & NGOS:
Preserving Wisdom for Generations

Africa is a deeply spiritual continent. From the earliest traditional councils to today's vibrant churches, mosques, and temples, faith has always been at the heart of African life. Alongside them, NGOs and community organisations have been documenting social challenges, health lessons, and grassroots victories for decades.

Together, these institutions carry vast treasures of wisdom, guidance, and lived experience. Yet much of it is oral, shared only in sermons, rituals, or reports that gather dust in filing cabinets. Imagine if these voices were systematically published into books, children's stories, family guides, or archives of moral wisdom. The impact would be immeasurable.

What Can Faith Institutions & NGOs Do?

- ✓ **Sermon Archives:** Transform years of teaching into books that inspire future generations.
- ✓ **Community Histories:** Document the growth of congregations, mosques, temples, and councils as part of cultural memory.

- ✓ **Moral & Family Guides:** Publish resources on parenting, relationships, and community values rooted in African spirituality.
- ✓ **Children's Literature:** Create storybooks that combine cultural heritage with moral lessons, in multiple languages.
- ✓ **NGO Case Studies:** Publish detailed casebooks of community projects that worked, what didn't so that others can replicate success.
- ✓ **Collaborations:** Partner with schools and universities to co-publish anthologies, health guides, or social impact stories.

What Are the Benefits?

- ➢ **Preserving Spiritual Heritage:** Oral sermons and teachings can easily be forgotten. Publishing preserves them for centuries.
- ➢ **Extending Influence Beyond the Pulpit:** A Sunday sermon may reach hundreds. A published book may reach tens of thousands.
- ➢ **Strengthening Families & Communities:** Books on faith, morality, and values can be passed down, anchoring generations in identity.
- ➢ **Credibility & Authority:** Published works give faith leaders and NGOs greater influence in policy debates, education, and interfaith dialogue.
- ➢ **Global Outreach:** Diaspora communities and global readers can access African faith

perspectives, countering stereotypes and enriching theology worldwide.

Imagine This

A church in Nigeria publishes a series of children's books on African proverbs and Bible stories in Yoruba, Igbo, and Hausa.

A mosque in Sudan collects and publishes centuries-old oral wisdom from its community elders, preserving traditions that might otherwise be lost.

A traditional council in Ghana publishes a guide to local rituals, explaining their meaning to younger generations.

An NGO in Malawi produces a book documenting its twenty years of work fighting malaria, creating a handbook for NGOs across Africa.

Now imagine 5,000 faith institutions and NGOs across the continent producing just **10 books per year**. That would add **50,000 titles annually,** many of which are filled with cultural and moral knowledge that no academic textbook can capture.

Beyond the numbers, the deeper impact is spiritual and cultural continuity. A book can carry the voice of a faith leader into the future long after they are gone. It can pass a tradition across borders. It can turn fleeting inspiration into lasting transformation.

Faith institutions and NGOs already shape millions of lives every day. Publishing multiplies that influence, making sure their wisdom outlives their buildings and their projects.

THE DIASPORA:
Bridging Worlds Through Story

The African diaspora is vast and powerful. An estimated **200 million Africans** live outside the continent, spread across Europe, the Americas, the Middle East, and Asia. This global family carries unique stories of migration, adaptation, resilience, and contribution. Yet, much of this experience remains undocumented.

The diaspora has a dual vantage point: it sees Africa through the lens of heritage, and the world through the lens of lived experience abroad. That position makes it uniquely capable of telling Africa's story to the world and the world's story back to Africa.

If even a small fraction of the diaspora committed to publishing, the results would be transformative.

<u>What Can the Diaspora Do?</u>

- ✓ **Personal Memoirs & Family Histories:** Document migration journeys, struggles, and successes. These become a heritage gift to future generations.
- ✓ **Children's Books:** Create stories that help diaspora children stay connected to their roots and languages.
- ✓ **Bridging Guides:** Write books that explain Africa to the world and the world to Africa manuals for trade, culture, or integration.

✓ **Publishing Platforms:** Diaspora entrepreneurs can set up publishing houses, magazines, or digital libraries to accelerate African content.

✓ **Funding & Mentorship:** Support writers back home by sponsoring projects, offering mentorship, and building distribution networks.

What Are the Benefits?

➢ **Identity & Legacy:** Published books keep African children in the diaspora rooted in their cultural heritage, preventing the erosion of identity.

➢ **Influence in Host Nations:** Diaspora books shape how host countries understand Africa, countering stereotypes and promoting respect.

➢ **Economic Opportunities:** Publishing opens revenue streams, book sales, speaking engagements, consulting, turning stories into wealth.

➢ **Bridging Africa & the World:** Diaspora voices connect cultures, opening pathways for trade, diplomacy, and collaboration.

➢ **Global African Presence:** A strong publishing contribution ensures Africa is visible in international research, AI, and cultural debates.

Imagine This

A Ugandan family in London publishes a memoir of their migration journey, becoming a reference for immigrant communities and policymakers.

A Ghanaian-American mother writes children's books about African heroes, giving diaspora kids role models beyond foreign superheroes.

A Nigerian tech entrepreneur in Silicon Valley documents lessons from building startups, inspiring young innovators across Africa.

A Somali community in Canada publishes oral histories of their elders, preserving traditions for generations.

If just one in every **5,000 diaspora Africans** published a book each year, that would result in approximately **40,000 new titles annually**. But their impact would go far beyond numbers. Diaspora publishing has the power to shift how Africa is perceived globally, to strengthen the self-worth of diaspora children, and to channel resources back into the continent.

The diaspora has always been Africa's bridge to the world. By publishing, it becomes Africa's amplifier, making sure that African perspectives are heard in every corner of the globe.

A Continental Vision: What a Published Africa Looks Like

Let us pause for a moment and imagine the future we are working toward.

Picture an Africa where a **million books are published every year,** not as a dream, but as a reality, where every village has at least one published author, where every secondary school contributes anthologies to the national library, and where every university produces textbooks rooted in African contexts. Where governments proudly publish their tribal languages, cultural histories, and policies.

Where corporations compete not only in profits but also in the number of books they have sponsored. Where faith institutions preserve moral wisdom in written form. Where the diaspora documents its journeys and builds bridges of knowledge across continents.

In Africa, our children will grow up seeing their realities reflected in classrooms. They will study from books written in their mother tongues. They will find themselves in the heroes and heroines of their own stories, not just imports.

In Africa, artificial intelligence will be trained not only on European or American data, but on African knowledge, values, and innovations. Algorithms will speak Kiswahili, Luganda, Hausa, Yoruba, Zulu, Amharic, and Wolof. AI will recognise African cultural references, cite African case studies, and reflect African thought.

In Africa, global negotiations will no longer be one-sided. When Africa walks into a room, it will not come empty-handed. It will bring a documented, published, and preserved record of its contributions, its innovations, its resources, and its philosophies. The continent's voice will be undeniable.

This is not a fantasy. It is a strategy. And it begins with publishing.

The Real Stakes: Publish or Perish

The choice before us is stark. If Africa does not publish, it will vanish from the future.

Artificial intelligence is not intelligent on its own. It only learns from what has been written. If Africa contributes only 2% of that knowledge, then 98% of the future's understanding of Africa will be shaped by outsiders. That means our histories could be rewritten, our innovations ignored, our cultures misrepresented, and our voices erased.

Think about this:

- ✧ If our land records are not documented, our ownership can be disputed.
- ✧ If our cultural rituals are not recorded, they can be misappropriated by others.
- ✧ If our research is not published, others will take credit for our discoveries.
- ✧ If our wisdom is not preserved, it will vanish with our elders.

Silence is not neutral; it is dangerous.

History shows us that nations rise and fall not only by their armies, but by their stories. The Roman Empire left records. The British Empire documented everything. Today, the United States dominates because it not only innovates but also publishes, distributes, and controls global knowledge.

If Africa remains under-documented, it will remain under-valued. And under-valuation is the first step toward exploitation.

But if we rise, if we move from 2% to 20%, we secure our place in the archives of humanity. We ensure that when the world asks questions about policy, culture, or science, Africa is not silent. We ensure that our children inherit not just land and wealth, but memory and identity.

Publishing is not optional. It is existential. It is survival. It is power.

The Final Call to Action: Your Role in Africa's Story

The question now is not whether Africa should publish, but whether **you** will play your part.

If you are an **individual**, write your story. Record your wisdom. Publish your experience. Do not wait for perfection. A simple book can carry your legacy for centuries.

If you are a **teacher or school leader**, guide your students to publish anthologies. Document your community's history. Make your school a contributor to Africa's archive.

If you are a **university professor or researcher**, do not let your findings die in unpublished papers. Turn them into books. Share them with communities. Put African scholarship on the global map.

If you are a **government leader**, invest in publishing as a national priority. Sponsor cultural histories, digitise archives, and ensure every ministry produces knowledge for the public. Protect your nation's memory by documenting it.

If you are a **corporate leader**, go beyond profit. Fund literacy projects. Publish guides for your industry. Leave a legacy that will outlast your balance sheets.

If you are a **faith leader**, do not let your sermons vanish into the air. Preserve them in books. Publish wisdom that will guide generations long after you are gone.

If you are part of the **diaspora**, tell your story. Write books for your children. Share your journey so the world can understand Africa through your eyes. Support writers back home. Fund platforms that accelerate content creation.

Africa needs every voice. Every book. Every effort.

Remember this: to reach half a million titles a year, we only need 1,300 books per day across 54 countries. That is not impossible. It is inevitable if we all act.

Conclusion: Write It Down or Watch It Disappear

Africa Is Not Poor—It Is Undocumented.

Africa Is Not Broken—It Is Unpublished.

Africa Is Not Behind—It Is Unheard.

That must end today.

The future will not remember Africa solely because of its population, its minerals, or its music. It will remember Africa if Africa documents itself.

The most powerful weapon in the world is not the bullet; it is the story. Nations that control the story control the future.

So let us not complain about being misrepresented while failing to represent ourselves. Let us not criticise the future if we refuse to prepare it with documented truth.

Whether you are a student or a CEO, a farmer or a minister, a poet or a programmer, your voice matters. Your story matters. Your knowledge matters.

You Don't Need Permission.
You Don't Need Perfection.
You Only Need to Begin.

Publishing Africa begins with publishing you.

This is your invitation:
Write Your Truth.
Publish Your Past.
Record Your Present.
Fund The Future.
Because if it is not documented, it does not exist.

And Africa must exist boldly, loudly, and permanently in the books, data, and algorithms that will shape the future.

CHAPTER TWELVE

BRIDGING THE DIVIDE: AFRICANS, AFRICAN-AMERICANS, AND AFRO-CARIBBEANS

"When we document ourselves, we not only preserve our past, we build the bridges that reconnect us to each other."

— Geoffrey Semaganda

One of the greatest tragedies of our global African story is not only what was stolen from us during slavery and colonialism, but also what we have failed to learn from one another since. The transatlantic slave trade ripped millions from the continent and scattered them across the Americas and the Caribbean.

Colonialism then carved up Africa, suppressing our languages, rewriting our histories, and forcing us to see ourselves through the eyes of others. For centuries, Africans on the continent, African-Americans in the United States, and Afro-Caribbeans across the islands and diaspora have lived like estranged relatives, members of one family who no longer recognize each other's faces.

Yet blood is thicker than borders. Whether in Lagos, Kingston, or Chicago, the drumbeat of Africa echoes in our music, our food, our faith, and our fight for dignity. Still, the knowledge we hold of one another has remained shallow, distorted, and filtered through foreign lenses. The colonizer's story has often been the only story we were taught about each other. Instead of learning each other's truths, we inherited caricatures.

The result is a dangerous ignorance. The average African child may grow up knowing little about the African-American journey how systemic racism, policies like Jim Crow, redlining, and mass incarceration created a generational wealth gap that still persists today. They may see images of successful African-American athletes and entertainers and assume the struggle is over, without understanding the structures that still hold millions back.

Meanwhile, many African-Americans know little of Africa beyond media portrayals of poverty, war, and corruption, unaware of the deep cultural resilience, natural wealth, and youthful innovation shaping the continent's future. Afro-Caribbeans, shaped by their own colonial histories of sugar plantations, indentured labour, and cultural hybridity, often find themselves caught in between bearing African roots but also Caribbean identities that are rarely fully acknowledged by either side.

When we do not know each other's stories, we fall prey to stereotypes. Africans may look down on African-Americans as people who "waste opportunities" in a land of plenty. African-Americans may dismiss Africans as "backward" or "naïve," assuming we live only in the shadows of poverty and underdevelopment. Afro-Caribbeans may feel erased altogether too often overlooked in both African and American narratives. These misunderstandings create invisible walls between us. And make no mistake: all of this division benefits no one but those who prefer us weak, divided, and silent.

The truth is this: we are far stronger together than apart. The genius of Africa, the resilience of African-Americans, and the creativity of Afro-Caribbeans are three branches of the same tree. Separated, we survive. United, we thrive.

Publishing Africa, therefore, is not just about documenting the continent. It is about documenting the entire African family. It is about reclaiming the narratives of Africans, African-Americans, and Afro-Caribbeans and weaving them together into a single, unstoppable force for dignity, wealth, and power.

This chapter matters because it is a call to end the estrangement. It is an invitation to look across the Atlantic and see our brothers and sisters, not as strangers, but as reflections of ourselves.

It is a declaration that we can no longer afford ignorance of one another, because ignorance robs us of opportunity, partnership, and destiny. To publish Africa is to publish us all our struggles, our triumphs, and our shared future.

The African-American Journey in Context

When I first began learning deeply about African-American history, I was shocked. Like many Africans, I had assumed that African-Americans simply lived in the world's richest country and should naturally be better off. I could not reconcile the image of America as the land of opportunity with the reality that the average Black household had only one-tenth the wealth of the average white household. For years, I accepted media stereotypes that poverty and struggle in Black America were the result of poor choices or lack of ambition.

Then I learned the truth: it was not laziness or lack of ambition. It was policy.

After the Civil War ended in 1865, freedom for formerly enslaved people came with chains of a different kind. Southern states passed vagrancy laws, which criminalized Black men for "not having a job" or for vague offenses like "mischief" or "insulting gestures."

Once arrested, these men were leased back to plantations, railroads, and mines in a system called convict leasing. Conditions were often worse than slavery, since employers had no long-term investment in the prisoners' health or survival. Men who had just been freed were effectively re-enslaved under law.

By the turn of the twentieth century, the rise of Jim Crow laws formalized racial segregation in schools, housing, hospitals, transportation, churches, restaurants, and even cemeteries. The message was clear: Black life was to be kept separate, inferior, and invisible.

When this system was challenged, courts often upheld it. In 1896, the U.S. Supreme Court's infamous Plessy v. Ferguson decision declared segregation legal under the doctrine of "separate but equal" though in reality, nothing was equal.

Even when African-Americans fought in World War I and World War II, returning veterans were denied the full benefits of service. The GI Bill, which created the modern American middle class by funding college education and home ownership, systematically excluded Black veterans through discriminatory lending practices and local administration.

From the 1930s to the 1960s, redlining a practice in which banks and the federal government marked Black neighbourhoods as "too risky" for investment kept Black families locked out of the housing market. Since homeownership was (and still is) the primary source of intergenerational wealth in America, this exclusion created a wealth gap that has never closed.

The mid-twentieth century brought progress through the Civil Rights Movement, with landmark victories like the 1954 *Brown v. Board of Education* decision that ended legal school segregation, and the 1964 Civil Rights Act that outlawed discrimination. Yet progress was met with backlash.

In the 1970s and 1980s, as deindustrialization stripped jobs from Black communities, the War on Drugs criminalized poverty and addiction. Harsh sentencing laws punished crack cocaine associated with Black neighbourhoods one hundred times more severely than powder cocaine, associated with white users. Police departments were militarized, no-knock raids became common, and incarceration rates for African-Americans skyrocketed.

Today, the United States imprisons a higher percentage of its Black population than South Africa did under apartheid. The consequences are devastating: broken families, generational poverty, and entire communities scarred by cycles of imprisonment and unemployment.

And yet, through all of this, African-Americans have continually produced cultural revolutions that reshaped not only America but the world. The Harlem Renaissance of the 1920s brought forth poets like Langston Hughes and thinkers like W.E.B. Du Bois. Jazz, blues, gospel, and later hip-hop became the soundtrack of global culture, rooted in African rhythms but uniquely shaped by the Black American experience.

The Civil Rights Movement of the 1960s gave us Martin Luther King Jr., Rosa Parks, Malcolm X, and countless unsung heroes whose courage redefined justice. Writers like Maya Angelou, James Baldwin, and Toni Morrison expanded the global imagination of Black identity. Leaders like Barack Obama showed the heights that could be reached, even against a backdrop of systemic disadvantage.

Understanding this context changes everything. It allows Africans and Afro-Caribbeans to see African-Americans not as people who "failed to thrive" in America, but as people who fought through impossible odds and still built legacies of influence. It reframes the narrative from deficiency to resilience. It reminds us that their story is not simply one of oppression, but of extraordinary creativity, courage, and contribution to the world.

When we, as Africans, finally see this truth, we stop asking, "Why haven't they done better?" and instead ask, "How did they achieve so much in spite of it all?" That shift from judgment to admiration, from ignorance to solidarity is the foundation for building bridges across the African world.

The Afro-Caribbean Story

The Caribbean is another vital chapter in our global African history a crossroads where Africa, Europe, and the Americas collided violently, and yet where some of the world's most powerful currents of resistance and creativity were born.

Millions of Africans were captured and shipped across the Atlantic during the transatlantic slave trade, and countless ships sailed into the harbours of Kingston, Port of Spain, Bridgetown, Havana, and Port-au-Prince carrying human cargo. Plantations in Jamaica, Trinidad, Barbados, Saint-Domingue (Haiti), and beyond were built on African labour. Sugar, rum, and tobacco flowed into European markets, generating unimaginable wealth for empires while enslaved Africans endured brutal conditions, high mortality rates, and constant dehumanization.

But the Caribbean story was never just one of victimhood. Resistance lived in the marrow of the people.

The Haitian Revolution of 1791 stands as a towering milestone in global history the first successful slave uprising that birthed the first free Black republic in the modern world. It was more than a rebellion; it was a declaration to humanity that freedom could not be permanently shackled. Haiti's victory sent shockwaves through slaveholding societies, terrifying colonial powers and inspiring enslaved people across the Americas.

Across other islands, Maroon communities escaped Africans who built settlements in the mountains and forests kept alive the spirit of defiance. In Jamaica, the Maroons fought guerrilla wars against the British and signed treaties that gave them a measure of autonomy. In Suriname, Maroon societies preserved African languages, drum rhythms, and spiritual practices, proving that even in exile, Africa survived.

When slavery was formally abolished in the nineteenth century, colonialism persisted in new forms. The Caribbean remained dominated by sugar economies, exploitative trade, and systems of indentured labour that brought workers from India and China into the region. The colonial rulers maintained political and economic control, keeping Afro-Caribbean populations marginalized and dependent.

The twentieth century brought the winds of independence, but not without struggle. Between the 1930s and the 1960s, waves of labour strikes, nationalist movements, and intellectual awakenings swept across the islands. Leaders like Eric Williams of Trinidad, Norman Manley of Jamaica, and Sir Grantley Adams of Barbados became architects of post-colonial self-determination. Yet independence came unevenly, and many small island nations remained economically vulnerable, tied to former colonial powers through debt, trade dependency, and tourism.

Migration became another defining feature of the Afro-Caribbean story. Large numbers moved to the United Kingdom during the Windrush era after World War II, responding to labour shortages. Others moved to Canada and the United States.

In these new lands, Afro-Caribbeans often faced the double burden of discrimination: as Black people within racist societies, and as immigrants navigating cultural differences. In Britain, Caribbean migrants endured hostility, housing discrimination, and employment barriers, yet their contributions helped rebuild the nation. In North America, they added vibrancy to cultural, academic, and political life while fighting for recognition and respect.

Despite these struggles, the Caribbean has gifted the world immense cultural treasures. Reggae, calypso, soca, zouk, and dancehall carried African rhythms into global consciousness. Through music, Afro-Caribbeans not only entertained but also resisted Bob Marley's reggae anthems were calls for justice, love, and liberation.

Literature and thought flourished through voices like Aimé Césaire, who advanced Negritude as a philosophy of Black pride; Derek Walcott, Nobel laureate poet who painted Caribbean landscapes with words; and Jamaica

Kincaid, whose novels exposed the complexities of colonial legacies.

Thinkers like Marcus Garvey ignited Pan-Africanism, calling for unity between Africa and its diasporas and inspiring movements from Harlem to Accra. Rastafarianism emerged as both a spiritual and political movement, rooting Black identity in Africa and proclaiming Ethiopia as Zion.

Afro-Caribbean identity is therefore profoundly hybrid, shaped by African roots, European colonial impositions, indigenous influences, and global migrations. It is creative, adaptive, and deeply tied to Africa, even when distance has blurred the lines. Caribbean festivals, food, and spirituality still echo Africa's imprint. Carnival, with its vibrant costumes and pulsating rhythms, is a living archive of African resistance wrapped in joy and artistry.

To understand Afro-Caribbean history is to understand that the African story did not stop at the shorelines of the continent. It continued across the sea, where Africans transformed oppression into art, bondage into resistance, and displacement into new cultural worlds.

The Caribbean shows us that African identity is not static but dynamic capable of survival, adaptation, and reinvention in any corner of the globe.

The Continental African Story

On the African continent, the story was no less brutal. In 1884–85, at the infamous Berlin Conference, European colonial powers sat around tables in faraway capitals and partitioned Africa as though carving up a pie, with little regard for cultures, communities, or centuries-old kingdoms.

Borders were drawn with rulers and pens, cutting through ethnic groups, splitting families, and joining together communities with little shared history. Ancient trade routes, political systems, and social bonds were ignored, replaced with artificial lines designed to serve Europe's appetite for land and resources.

For nearly a century, Africa endured the weight of colonial domination. Europeans extracted minerals, oil, and agricultural wealth while suppressing indigenous governance and rewriting African identity in textbooks and laws. Africans were told their languages were inferior, their spirituality was superstition, their histories were myths. Generations grew up in systems where their heritage was erased and their worth defined by their utility to empire.

The independence movements of the mid-20th century brought new hope. Across the continent, young leaders rose to declare freedom: Kwame Nkrumah in Ghana, Jomo Kenyatta in Kenya, Patrice Lumumba in Congo, Julius Nyerere in Tanzania. Flags were raised, constitutions written, and a wave of optimism swept from Cape Town to Cairo. Africa seemed poised to reclaim its destiny.

But liberation was quickly complicated. The Cold War turned Africa into a chessboard for foreign powers. The U.S. and the Soviet Union, more interested in ideology and influence than African self-determination, fuelled coups, funded rebellions, and propped up dictators.

Promising leaders like Lumumba were assassinated or deposed, while strongmen willing to serve foreign interests were armed and empowered.

By the 1970s and 1980s, Structural Adjustment Programs (SAPs) imposed by the International Monetary Fund and World Bank crippled many African economies. In exchange for loans, governments were forced to privatize industries, slash public spending, and open markets to foreign competition.

Schools, hospitals, and social services suffered. Meanwhile, multinational corporations continued to siphon off Africa's resource wealth diamonds, oil, cobalt, cocoa leaving communities impoverished while profits flowed abroad.

Yet Africa is not only a story of exploitation. It is also a story of resilience and rebirth. Today, Africa stands at a crossroads. It is the world's youngest continent, with a median age under twenty and a population projected to reach 2.5 billion by 2050. Its soil is fertile, its minerals critical for the global digital economy, and its sun powerful enough to light the world through renewable energy.

Its cities from Nairobi to Lagos, Kigali to Accra are buzzing with startups, innovation hubs, and cultural revolutions in music, fashion, and film. Afrobeats fills stadiums, Nollywood films dominate streaming platforms, and African tech entrepreneurs are raising billions in investment.

And yet, poverty, weak institutions, and external dependency remain. Many governments still rely heavily on aid or resource exports. Corruption undermines trust. Infrastructures lag behind population growth. For many young Africans, opportunity feels far away, leading to migration, brain drain, or disillusionment.

The tragedy is compounded by a lack of knowledge about the wider African family. Many Africans themselves grow up with little understanding of diaspora struggles. School curricula often stop at colonial history and independence, rarely covering the Civil Rights Movement, Caribbean independence leaders, or the systemic racism faced by Black communities in the West.

This absence leaves many Africans vulnerable to stereotypes. Some assume that African-Americans are "lazy" or "spoiled," unable to succeed despite living in wealthy nations. Others fail to recognize the unique creativity and hybrid strength of Afro-Caribbean identity.

This ignorance cuts both ways. Africans miss out on learning from the strategies of resilience that diaspora communities developed under oppression. Diaspora communities miss out on seeing Africa as a continent of opportunity rather than a place of despair. The walls between us are built not only by history but by silence, by unshared stories.

The continental African story, therefore, cannot be told in isolation. It must be woven together with the journeys of African-Americans and Afro-Caribbeans. Only then can we see the full picture: a global African family that has endured slavery, colonialism, and racism, yet continues to rise, innovate, and create.

Myths and Misunderstandings

For centuries, Africans, African-Americans, and Afro-Caribbeans have been fed stories about each other that are incomplete at best and poisonous at worst. These myths often go unchallenged, passed down casually in conversations, reinforced by biased media portrayals, and cemented by the absence of deliberate cross-education. Without realizing it, we begin to see each other not as brothers and sisters, but as caricatures.

Africans may think, *"At least we were never enslaved in America."*

This view ignores the devastation of colonialism, which stripped Africa of land, labour, and autonomy. It also trivializes the enduring pain of the transatlantic slave trade, which tore millions from the continent in the first place. By saying this, some Africans position themselves as "luckier" or "purer," forgetting that the chains of empire were only different in form, not in cruelty.

African-Americans may think, *"At least we don't live in poverty like Africans."*

This perspective often grows out of media images that present Africa as a continent of famine, war, and corruption, without showing its thriving cities, resilient cultures, and growing economies. It overlooks the fact that poverty exists in every society, including the United States, and that Africa's wealth in resources, youth, and creativity makes it a land of enormous potential.

Afro-Caribbeans may feel invisible, overlooked by both sides. Too often, the Caribbean is left out of the conversation.

Africans and African-Americans may focus on their direct experiences while neglecting the unique hybrid story of the Caribbean its Maroon warriors, independence struggles, and cultural revolutions. This erasure can leave Afro-Caribbeans feeling like outsiders in a family they fully belong to.

Each of these myths is built not on truth, but on silence and stereotypes. The media has often been the most powerful storyteller, presenting Africa as "backward," African-Americans as "violent" or "criminal," and Afro-Caribbeans as exotic entertainers rather than intellectual contributors. These images, repeated enough times, begin to feel real even to us.

The tragedy is not just that outsiders misrepresent us, but that we internalize these lies and turn them against one another. Africans sometimes mock African-Americans for their struggles. African-Americans sometimes mock Africans for accents or cultural practices. Afro-Caribbeans sometimes distance themselves from both, fearing association with negative stereotypes. In each case, division deepens while dignity erodes.

The truth is that none of us are superior to the other. We are three branches of the same tree, each scarred by history but still rooted in Africa's soil.

The myths we believe about one another are not reflections of who we are they are the consequences of centuries of disconnection. To break them, we must replace silence with stories, stereotypes with scholarship, and suspicion with solidarity.

What We Gain by Learning Each Other's Stories

When we document and share our narratives, everything shifts. Knowledge becomes the antidote to suspicion, and connection becomes the cure for division. Each story told across oceans stitches us closer together, reminding us that we are not strangers but family.

The benefits of this reconnection are immense.

Solidarity

African-Americans fighting against systemic racism and police brutality gain strength when Africans and Afro-Caribbeans stand with them, recognizing that their struggle is part of our shared history of resistance. Likewise, when Africans on the continent push for fair trade, climate justice, or freedom from exploitative global contracts, the voices of diaspora communities become powerful amplifiers.

Solidarity turns local struggles into global movements, giving us collective leverage that no single group could wield alone.

Economics

Today, remittances from the diaspora to Africa exceed $100 billion annually greater than all foreign aid combined. Yet this money often flows informally, sustaining families but rarely transforming economies. Imagine if this wealth were channelled strategically into infrastructure, startups, educational institutions, and cultural industries.

Diaspora capital, paired with Africa's raw opportunity, could create a cycle of growth and prosperity that would dwarf foreign aid dependency. This is the hidden economic engine of Pan-African collaboration, waiting to be unlocked.

Culture

The blending of African, African-American, and Afro-Caribbean creativity has already reshaped global culture. Jazz, reggae, hip-hop, Afrobeats, dancehall, Nollywood, and literature from Toni Morrison to Derek Walcott all spring from different corners of the African family.

But what happens when we intentionally collaborate instead of coincidentally intersecting? With unity, we could build industries that rival Hollywood, Silicon Valley, or the European art capitals cultural economies rooted in African values, funded by African wealth, and celebrated by African pride.

Technology

The diaspora holds immense expertise in technology, medicine, education, and entrepreneurship, often gained through generations of navigating advanced economies. At the same time, Africa's youthful population is pioneering innovation with limited resources, creating mobile banking systems, health apps, and renewable energy solutions admired worldwide.

When these streams merge diaspora knowledge meeting African ingenuity, we do not just catch up with the rest of the world. We set the pace. The next frontier of technology could carry an African accent.

Pathways to Reconnection

For all of this potential to be realized, we must move beyond wishful thinking. Reconnection requires intentional pathways bridges we build across oceans, cultures, and generations.

Publishing

The first pathway is the one closest to our hearts: publishing. Books, documentaries, podcasts, oral archives, and digital platforms that tell our stories side by side are more than information they are identity.

When an African child reads the autobiography of Malcolm X, or an African-American student watches a documentary about Nkrumah's Pan-African dream, the wall of ignorance begins to crack. Publishing ensures our voices do not vanish but instead echo across time and space.

Education

Schools must take responsibility for telling the full African story. In Africa, students should learn about the Civil Rights Movement, the Harlem Renaissance, and Caribbean independence heroes with the same seriousness as their own independence struggles. In the Americas and the Caribbean, curricula must highlight Africa beyond slavery teaching about Mali's golden age, Ethiopia's resilience, and Africa's current innovation.

Education is how we raise a generation that sees each other as equals and allies, not as mysteries or stereotypes.

Festivals and Exchanges

Culture is the most joyful bridge we can build. Pan-African festivals of music, literature, and film create spaces where Africans, African-Americans, and Afro-Caribbeans meet face-to-face, collaborate, and celebrate shared heritage.

Exchange programs student visits, artist residencies, academic partnerships help people experience one another's realities directly. Every dance performed, every poem recited, every idea shared across borders is a stitch in the fabric of unity.

Business

Commerce can be just as transformative as culture. Diaspora investment tours, startup accelerators, and incubation hubs on the continent can bring capital, mentorship, and market access to African entrepreneurs.

Likewise, African markets can open doors for diaspora businesses to expand and thrive. Business partnerships shift our relationship from charity to shared prosperity where both sides benefit and build wealth together.

Faith and Family

Finally, we cannot ignore the power of spiritual and familial bonds. Churches, mosques, and traditional spiritual centres have always been spaces of gathering and identity. They can become platforms for reconnection, where African theological thought, Caribbean spiritual resilience, and African-American gospel traditions enrich one another.

Families, too, hold power: genealogy projects, family reunions, and ancestral tracing allow people in the diaspora to rediscover their African roots, while Africans rediscover the global branches of their family tree.

When we build these pathways publishing, education, festivals, business, and faith we begin to heal centuries of separation. We move from fragmented voices to a choir, from scattered sparks to a blaze, from isolated struggles to a shared destiny.

The Role of Documentation

Every story we document becomes a bridge. Every archive becomes an anchor. Without documentation, our histories drift like ships without harbours easily lost, easily rewritten, easily dismissed. With documentation, we create maps that guide future generations back to their roots and forward into their possibilities.

Publishing Africa must therefore mean publishing not only Africa, but also the diaspora. The African story is incomplete if it stops at the shores of the continent. It stretches across the Atlantic, where it took root in plantations and parishes, in Harlem streets and Caribbean hillsides, in gospel choirs and reggae stages.

To document Africa is to document the whole African world, in all its diversity, struggle, and creativity.

Tools of Connection

Documentation can take many forms:

- ♦ Oral histories that capture the voices of elders before they fall silent, ensuring that proverbs, family stories, and wisdom are not lost.
- ♦ Family memoirs that turn personal experiences into generational guides, reminding children and grandchildren of who they are and where they come from.
- ♦ Cultural anthologies that gather poetry, music, fashion, and folklore into volumes that celebrate shared heritage.
- ♦ Blockchain-protected archives that secure intellectual property, giving Africans and the diaspora ownership of their narratives in an age of digital exploitation.

Each form is a tool for connection. Each record is a reminder that we exist, that we matter, and that we belong to one another.

The Transformative Power of Reading Each Other

When Africans read African-American memoirs narratives of resilience in the face of segregation, mass incarceration, and systemic inequality they learn empathy. They begin to see that survival in America required not weakness but extraordinary strength.

When African-Americans study African independence struggles Nkrumah's Pan-African vision, Mandela's resilience, Sankara's bold reforms they rediscover pride. They realize that Africa is not simply a place of despair as too often portrayed, but a continent of courage and creativity.

When Afro-Caribbeans publish their hybrid heritage drawing threads from Africa, Europe, and indigenous traditions they remind us of our unity. They show that African identity is not fragile but expansive, capable of adapting, resisting, and reinventing itself across oceans and generations.

From Division to Destiny

Documentation dismantles stereotypes. It replaces silence with testimony, suspicion with understanding, and ignorance with truth. It allows us to see not only what divides us, but what binds us. When our stories are written, recorded, archived, and shared, they become collective memory and collective strategy.

The role of documentation is not simply to preserve the past. It is to prepare the future. Every documented story is a resource for teaching, a weapon against erasure, and a blueprint for collaboration.

When we publish our memories, we are not just remembering we are *re-membering*, bringing the scattered parts of the African family back together as one body.

A Vision of Unity

Unity is not a dream too fragile to hold; it is a vision waiting for deliberate action. Across the African world, the possibilities are endless when we choose to know, honour, and publish one another's stories.

Imagine a child in Lagos learning about Malcolm X alongside Nelson Mandela not as separate figures from different continents, but as co-architects of freedom whose words still echo across the globe. The lesson is no longer African history or African-American history, but *African world history.*

Imagine a student in Chicago studying Yoruba cosmology alongside Martin Luther King Jr.'s sermons. In that classroom, spiritual wisdom from West Africa and prophetic vision from the American South are not strangers, but partners in shaping a new moral imagination. Faith and culture, once divided by oceans, are reunited as sources of dignity.

Imagine a Jamaican teenager publishing a book that links island folklore to Ghanaian traditions. She begins to see her grandmother's Anansi stories not just as Caribbean tales but as echoes of Akan heritage. Through her pen, the Atlantic ceases to be a barrier and becomes a bridge, tying Kingston to Kumasi.

Imagine Pan-African festivals where musicians from Accra, poets from Harlem, and dancers from Port of Spain collaborate on stages that celebrate both difference and connection.

Imagine digital platforms where elders in Uganda, pastors in Detroit, and storytellers in Barbados upload their wisdom into one shared archive. Imagine marketplaces where African crafts meet diaspora design, and diaspora technology fuels African enterprise.

This is not fantasy. It is possible, if we publish ourselves and each other. Unity is not built on sentiment alone it is built on knowledge. When we share our narratives, we collapse the distance between us. We move from fragmented histories to a single, powerful testimony: that no matter where the ships carried us, no matter what borders were drawn, we remain one people.

A vision of unity means more than coexistence; it means collaboration. It means Africans, African-Americans, and Afro-Caribbeans lifting each other up, investing in one another's futures, and standing together in global conversations about justice, economics, and culture. It means the world no longer sees us as scattered voices but as a chorus, speaking with the authority of history and the confidence of destiny.

And the key is simple but profound: publish. Publish the poems, the sermons, the proverbs, the policies, the archives, the testimonies. Publish until no African child grows up ignorant of their cousins across the ocean. Publish until no African-American or Afro-Caribbean sees Africa only through poverty-stricken images. Publish until unity is no longer a dream but a daily reality.

Conclusion: One Story, Many Journeys

We cannot afford to remain ignorant of one another. The stakes are too high. One in every five human beings on this planet is African or of African descent. Together, we represent more than a billion voices, more than a billion dreams, more than a billion untapped opportunities.

And yet, if this vast community remains divided, suspicious, and disconnected, then the world will continue to prosper at our expense while we remain on the margins of power.

The cure is within our reach. Publishing is the cure. By publishing our histories, we publish our humanity. By documenting our journeys, we dismantle stereotypes. By learning each other's stories, we rebuild the bridges that slavery, colonialism, and systemic racism tried to burn.

Publishing is more than printing it is a form of power. It allows us to say to the world: *we are here, we matter, and we define ourselves.* Africans on the continent, African-Americans in the United States, and Afro-Caribbeans across the islands are not three separate peoples we are three expressions of one story, three branches of the same tree. Each has faced storms. Each has borne scars. And each has produced fruit that nourishes the world.

When we unite these journeys, we create something unstoppable. Solidarity replaces suspicion. Respect replaces rivalry. Collaboration replaces competition. Together we transform the narrative of being the world's most exploited people into becoming the world's most innovative force.

"The best opportunity for Africans everywhere is on the African continent. But only when we document, only when we learn, only when we respect, will we truly seize it."

— Geoffrey Semaganda

So, let us tell the story in its fullness: Africa, African-America, and the Afro-Caribbean. Let us publish every poem, every proverb, every testimony, every triumph. Let us ensure that no African child grows up blind to the struggles of their cousins abroad, and no diaspora child grows up seeing Africa only through the eyes of outsiders.

The time for silence has passed. The time for disconnection has ended. The time for publishing has come.

Let us replace ignorance with knowledge.

Let us replace rivalry with respect.

Let us replace division with destiny.

For we are not three stories we are one story, told in many voices, across many journeys. And when we learn to hear each other, we will finally remember who we are: one family, one future, one Africa.

CONCLUSION

WRITE IT DOWN OR BE WRITTEN OUT

Africa stands at a crossroads. On one side lies silence, an inherited silence from colonial erasure, systemic under-documentation, and generational loss. On the other side lies authorship, A path toward reclaiming our memory, restoring our dignity, and shaping our place in the global future. This book has been an urgent invitation to choose the latter, not with hesitation but with bold, coordinated action.

We have travelled through Africa's oral traditions, its intellectual property crisis, its undervalued creative industries, its diaspora disconnect, and its underfunded archives. We have exposed the hidden costs of our continent's under-documentation from cultural loss to economic exclusion, from generational disconnect to AI invisibility.

But more important, we have imagined a different future, one where Africans tell their own stories, in their own voices, using every format the world offers and even inventing a few of our own.

Publishing Africa is not just a book title. It is a mandate. It is the call of our ancestors whose names were never written down. It is the echo of our youth scrolling through a digital world where their identity is missing. It is the cry of our continent, a place of undeniable contribution and yet unacknowledged documentation.

Why This Mission Matters Now More Than Ever

We live in an era where information determines power. What's documented becomes part of the algorithm. What's cited shapes policy. What's searchable becomes truth. And what's visible earns respect, capital, and continuity. In such a world, Africa cannot afford to be undocumented.

Publishing is no longer optional. It is strategic. It is generational. It is existential.

If we fail to publish our stories, we risk raising generations who know more about medieval Europe than ancient Mali, more about Western saints than African sages, more about Shakespeare than Sankara. We risk becoming guests in our own history, silenced by the absence of text, footage, and verified cultural data.

But when we document, everything changes. We gain leverage. We inspire pride. We create economies. We educate the future not with borrowed identity, but with our own.

Lessons from This Journey

Over the chapters, we've discovered that publishing is not limited to books. It is a dynamic, multi-format act of remembrance, empowerment, and transformation.

Whether through videos, podcasts, museum exhibits, TikTok dances, school essays, oral recordings, or VR installations, publishing is simply the intentional act of making truth visible, transferable, and preserved.

We've explored how:

- ⬥ **Documentation is wealth:** Not just cultural or intellectual, but economic. When we record, we own. When we own, we can trade, teach, and transmit value.
- ⬥ **Every African is a publisher:** Whether a child recording their grandmother's song, a pastor writing sermons, or a farmer documenting soil rituals, every voice counts.
- ⬥ **Institutions must lead:** From governments to faith organisations, from schools to tech startups, we need ecosystems that make publishing scalable, respected, and rewarded.
- ⬥ **The diaspora must reconnect intellectually:** It is no longer enough to send remittances. We must send back ideas, support content creation, and invest in memory.
- ⬥ **The youth are not waiting:** They are already creating content. The question is whether we will train, fund, and guide them or continue to ignore their role as modern scribes.
- ⬥ **Faith, identity, and culture must be preserved:** Without documentation, African spirituality is demonised, African families are fragmented, and African morals are weakened.

✧ **The future is AI, and AI needs African data:** If Africa remains underrepresented in global databases, AI will misinterpret, exclude, and misrepresent us. The machines of tomorrow must learn from us, not just about us.

This is why publishing Africa is a *civilizational responsibility* one we can no longer defer to external voices or future generations.

A Pan-African Effort for a Pan-African Future

This book has offered blueprints for action: from the Action Wealth Publishing Model to community storytelling hubs, from youth publishing camps to a continental fund for African content creators. But none of it will matter unless each of us takes ownership.

Publishing Africa must become a collaborative, cross-sector mission:

➢ **Governments must legislate memory:** Documentation should be a public good, not a personal luxury. National libraries, translation initiatives, cultural protection laws, and publishing subsidies are necessary investments in national identity.

➢ **Philanthropists and donors must act with urgency:** Funding storytelling, language preservation, and cultural technology is as vital as funding infrastructure because infrastructure without memory is a skeleton.

- **Universities must republish Africa:** Curriculum reform, local textbook creation, and research funding must anchor education in our context and history.
- **Faith centres must preserve moral narratives:** Our spiritual wisdom must be printed, sung, coded, and shared, not left behind in oral fragments alone.
- **Media houses and publishers must innovate and include.** From multilingual formats to audio-first platforms, we must meet people where they are, not just where the elite reside.
- **Diaspora must invest in return legacies:** Not just in flights and homes, but in publishing their migration experiences, their parents' memories, and their cultural reflections.
- **The private sector must see publishing as CSR:** Content is brand. Supporting local creators, documenting corporate impact, and publishing African innovation strengthens both society and company identity.
- **The youth must lead:** They are already producing. They now need mentorship, tools, funding, and trust.

No movement becomes history until it is written. No voice echoes unless it is amplified.

If We Don't Publish, We Perish Politically, Economically, Spiritually

The cost of not documenting Africa is already being felt. Languages are disappearing. Outsiders are patenting traditional knowledge. African children are growing up thinking that value lies elsewhere. AI is being trained on everyone else's worldview. Our absence in the written record is costing us power at every table.

Silence is not passive. It is complicit. But it doesn't have to be this way.

We can choose a new future for a documented Africa. An Africa that writes itself into the textbooks, the algorithms, the archives, and the imagination of the world. An Africa that no longer waits to be published but takes the pen, the camera, the microphone, the laptop, and says: *This is who we are. This is what we've contributed. This is where we're going.*

We can train scribes in every village. Build archives in every region. Create apps that preserve local dialects. Animate stories in classrooms. Turn community ceremonies into cultural curricula. Elevate storytellers as national treasures. And ensure that no memory, no name, no lesson is lost to silence.

A Final Word

I did not write this book as a critic of Africa. I wrote it as a son of the continent, a believer in her beauty, her depth, her resilience. I wrote it as someone who has seen what happens when we are undocumented, and what becomes possible when we own our voice.

This is not a perfect book. But it is a sincere offering, a spark, a map, a mirror. A reminder that we are not poor, we are unpublished. We are not voiceless, we are unheard. We are not lost, we are just unwritten.

But not anymore.

The pen is in our hands. The mic is on. The archive is open.

Now is the time.

Write it down. Record it. Translate it. Publish it.

Before we are forgotten.

So that we will be remembered.

And so that our grandchildren will never again question where they come from, who they are, or what their people contributed to the world.

ABOUT

GEOFFREY SEMAGANDA

Entrepreneur | Author | Publisher | Visionary

Geoffrey Semaganda is an entrepreneur, author, publisher, and philanthropist whose journey from Uganda to the global stage has inspired and impacted more than 500,000 people across 65 countries.

With a career spanning over thirty years, he has transformed the business and personal development sectors by turning ideas into assets, stories into influence, and expertise into legacy.

As the founder of Action Wealth Group, Geoffrey has empowered over 750 authors and businesses and developed more than 2,000 training and publishing programs worldwide.

He has personally published eight business books and more than twenty training programs, while building systems that enable individuals, communities, and institutions to document their knowledge, monetise their expertise, and preserve their heritage.

He spearheads the **Publishing Africa** initiative**,** a platform and movement created to address the continent's chronic under-documentation and to ensure African voices are preserved, celebrated, and represented in global systems, including artificial intelligence. He is also pioneering a blockchain-based publishing and knowledge-sharing platform designed to fuel both profit and non-profit initiatives, with a special focus on empowering Africa.

Geoffrey's entrepreneurial journey began as a teenager in London, where he launched his first business at the age of sixteen and expanded into multiple ventures across Europe by the time he was twenty-one. Born in Uganda, he embodies resilience, adaptability, and the spirit of cross-cultural leadership. His path from surviving the challenges of a war-torn homeland to mentoring CEOs and advising government ministries reflects both his grit and his global perspective.

Guided by his core belief, *"If it's not documented, it doesn't exist,"* Geoffrey has dedicated his life to helping people capture their knowledge, share their stories, and build systems that will outlive them. His work blends cutting-edge publishing technology with cultural sensitivity, positioning him as a leading voice on knowledge equity, cultural preservation, and economic empowerment through publishing.

Beyond business, Geoffrey is a husband, father, mentor, and speaker whose message resonates across faith, education, and entrepreneurship. His charitable initiatives focus on youth empowerment, clean water access, and blood donation campaigns.

Whether addressing an international conference, leading a workshop, or building platforms for underrepresented voices, he remains committed to a singular vision: shaping Africa's future one published voice at a time.

www.ingramcontent.com/pod-product-compliance
Lightning Source LLC
Chambersburg PA
CBHW020831160426
43192CB00007B/608